The Man Between the Ears

STAR TREK'S
LEONARD NIMOY

PITTSBURGH
PUBLIC
THEATER

JAMES VAN HISE

OTHER PIONEER BOOKS

- •FILMS OF BRUCE LEE by Edward Gross
- •WHO WAS THAT MASKED MAN? by James Van His
- •PAUL MCCARTNEY: 20 YRS ON HIS OWN by Edward Gros
- •DARK SHADOWS TRIBUTE BOOK by Gross & Van Hise
- •UNOFFICIAL BEAUTY AND THE BEAST by Edward Gross
- •TREK: THE LOST YEARS by Edward Gross
- •THE TREK ENCYCLOPEDIA by John Peel
- •HOW TO DRAW FOR COMIC BOOKS by James Van Hise
- •THE TREK CREW BOOK by James Van Hise
- •BATMANIA by James Van Hise
- •GUNSMOKE by John Pee
- •ELVIS-THE MOVIES by Hal Schuster
- •ODD COUPLE COMPANION by Edward Gross
- •UNOFFICIAL MAKING OF A WISEGUY by Edward Gross
- •TWIN PEAKS: BEHIND THE SCENES by Mark Altman
- •WONDER YEARS by Ed Gross
- •HOW TO CREATE ANIMATION by John Cawley &Jim Korkis
- •25TH ANNIV. TREK CELEBRATION by James Van Hise
- •THE LA LAW BOOK by Edward Gross
- •THE ROCKFORD PHILE by David Martindale
- •ZZ TOP by Scott Nance
- •FUNNY STUFF by James Van Hise
- •LIFE WITH THE BEATLES by Alistair Taylor & Hal Schuster
- •DEANMANIA by Robert Headrick, Jr.
- •ADDAM'S FAMILY by James Van Hise
- •VIDEO SUPERHEROES by James Van Hise
- •PERRY MASON CASEBOOK by David Martindale
- •THE WOODY ALLEN ENCYCLOPEDIA by Mark Altman
- •HISTORY OF TREK by James Van Hise
- •CHEERS by James Van Hise
- •CARTOON SUPERSTARS by John Cawley &Jim Korkis
- •TREK FAN HANDBOOK by James Van Hise
- •NEW KIDS by Scott Nance
- •LOST IN SPACE TRIBUTE by James Van Hise

Designed and Edited by Hal Schuster

Library of Congress Cataloging-in-Publication Data
James Van Hise, 1949—
         The Man Between the Ears: Star Trek's Leonard Nimoy

         1. The Man Between the Ears: Star Trek's Leonard Nimoy (television)
   I. Title

Published by Pioneer Books, Inc., 5715 N. Balsam Rd., Las Vegas, NV, 89130.

First Printing, 1992

Introduction

Leonard Nimoy. It is, perhaps, impossible to hear that name or see that face without immediately thinking about. . . well, that *other* guy. The logical fellow with the pointed ears. In other words, Mr. Spock. Indeed, some are so adamant in their association of the two that they seem to think that the character created the actor and not the other way around.

This book will redress this tragicomic imbalance by showing just how far Leonard Nimoy had to travel before a lucky stroke of casting propelled him to international fame. Indeed, it will show that while Mr. Nimoy's career might have been made by his Vulcan alter ego, it was the talented Mr. Nimoy who made Spock, and all that is associated with him, a shining success. The wrong actor might have made a hash of the role and consigned *Star Trek* to the dustbin of oblivion; it took Nimoy, with twenty-five years of acting and struggle behind him, to make the world believe in such a radically new character. . . and on a weekly basis, to boot.

His keen mind and his dedication to his craft are what really made Leonard Nimoy a success. As will be demonstrated, he started early and had to work a long time before fame became his. Then he refused to rest on his laurels. True, association with his most famous creation might have been a stumbling block at times, but his persistence and honest dedication always cleared the way for new and varied projects on the stage, fine dramatic portrayals for television and in film, and even a second major career as a highly-acclaimed film director. All this, with some fine professional still photography and a growing number of poetic volumes, thrown in for good measure. Not one to be idle, Leonard Nimoy has always kept himself busy with his work and interests, and his energies show no sign of flagging.

This is the story of what he's done. . . so far.

Boston

Leonard Nimoy was born in Boston, Massachusetts on March 3rd, 1931, the son of Jewish immigrants from the Ukraine. He grew up in the West End, where his father, Max, ran a barber shop, and was raised in the faith of his ancestors, a worldview which still guides Leonard's approach to life.

He still speaks Yiddish, the language he learned as a child. The young Leonard was also greatly impressed by the magical world of the movies, and recalls being moved to tears by Charles Laughton's portrayal of Quasimodo in the 1939 version of *The Hunchback of Notre Dame*. At a very early age, he demonstrated the ability to memorize entire poems, which he would then read to his entire class at school. Although he was nervous doing this, it gave him a sense of accomplishment. Throughout his education, he was often involved in public performances. When he saw his first play— Gilbert and Sullivan's "HMS Pinafore"— at a neighborhood theater, he was hooked on acting, and soon appeared, at the age of nine, in a production of the children's opera "Hansel and Gretel. " Since he lived a mere three blocks away from the small community theater, he got the role almost by accident.

"I was raised in the West End," Nimoy recalled in a 1987 interview in the *Boston Sunday Herald*. "We lived on Chambers Street. My father had a barber shop on Leverett. I used to spend my time after school at the Elizabeth Peabody House, at 357 Charles. It was supported by community funds and philanthropies. They had a science lab and a basketball court. They also taught various classes in arts and crafts. One day I was hanging out and someone said, 'Can you sing?' I sang 'God Bless America,' and the next thing I knew, I was playing Hansel in 'Hansel and Gretel.' I was 8. That's how it started. Boston has always been a great city for presenting opportunities for kids. I felt I came from a rich environment."

While his interest in performing occupied much of his time, he was also involved in a wide variety of youthful pastimes, including basketball, fencing and

photography. At the age of fifteen, he constructed a homemade enlarger from inexpensive parts, and embarked on a brief career doing candid portraits of neighborhood children. Many years later, he would take up photography again in earnest—but for the time being, his interest in acting began to take precedence.

Other than acting, Nimoy was an average student, who often felt out of place in classes. This was not helped by the fact that he had a "brilliant" older brother who excelled at everything; Leonard often felt awkward and inadequate by comparison. Once he even asked a chemistry teacher to give him a passing grade he didn't really deserve, explaining that he would never utilize chemistry in real life, and that the grade would certainly not be misused to lay the foundations for a fraudulent career in science later in life. The teacher bought this convoluted philosophical argument and gave him the passing grade.

A temple production of the play "The Man Who Hated God" first brought Leonard into contact with Elliot Silverstein, the show's director. Silverstein would eventually direct him in a number of plays, as would fellow Bostonian Boris Sagal, who directed the 17-year-old Leonard as Bobby Randall in a production of Clifford Odets' "Awake And Sing." This was the last role Nimoy recalls performing in Boston. Remembering that time, he said, "There was a director named Boris Sagal who staged plays at the settlement house in exchange for room and board. I did plays there—Chekhov, Ibsen, Strindberg. I was a very serious guy in those days. I thought comedy was frivolous. I didn't want to be bothered by it. I was given a summer scholarship to study drama at Boston College by Father Bonn. That was the first time someone had validated me as an actor."

Both Silverstein and Sagal would later reappear in the course of Leonard's career.

In the course of performing in "Awake And Sing," Leonard found himself being drawn toward the theater as a vocation. Years later he would look back on the experience and tell *The New York Times* (10/30/88), "I was sent reeling. I was playing the troubled teenager. I was a troubled teenager. I thought, 'I've got to do this the rest of my life. "

Leonard's parents were not too thrilled by the prospect of their son pursuing an acting career, but he followed his own desires. As the Nimoys' second child, Leonard had been raised in the shadow of his older brother; this was his way of asserting his individuality. Even so, he seemed for years to favor secondary roles, and even once claimed to have been somewhat embarrassed when *Star Trek* made him famous.

In addition to taking an active part in community and temple theater productions, the energetic teenager performed with amateur singing groups in local movie houses, a ploy beleaguered theater owners had recently adopted to fight television's growing pull on the movie audience. He also became involved in a radio program sponsored by the B'nai B'rith, a Jewish fraternal organization, taking roles in radio sketches. It would still be quite a while before he broke into the new medium of television.

Throughout the rest of the 1940s, he learned the thespian's craft, and appeared in numerous stage productions at Temple Mishkan Tefila, Boston College's Summer Theater and at the theater where he had made his youthful acting debut as Hansel, the Elizabeth Peabody Playhouse.

After finishing high school, Leonard enrolled in Boston College on a two-month summer scholarship program, where he became involved in an intensive theater course, which gave him an opportunity to work in various positions in productions that were mounted with little pause for relaxation. He didn't stick with it, however; when he'd finally saved up seven hundred dollars from his various jobs, he spent one hundred dollars on a train ticket and headed for California. Jokingly, he claimed he wanted to become a famous actor to show up all the jocks who got all the girls instead of him!

His parents were dubious about this decision. They enjoyed his acting, but, as his mother Dora later recalled, "Leonard was a good boy, but he was no student, like Melvin [his brother] . . . . He was very good about working, though . . . . earned his own money since he was eleven. He liked acting even then. Of course, Max and I didn't take it seriously. He broke our hearts when he quit college at seventeen and went to California to study acting, but now we're very proud."

At the time, however, his chosen course of action left his future very uncertain—but the stagestruck teenager knew what he wanted to do, and was not the least bit deterred from pursuing his heart's desire.

2 Welcome to LA

Leonard Nimoy went to Los Angeles the long and difficult way, by train, surviving on junk food along the three-day cross-continental journey. "I had started out with a love of the theater," he later stated, "but came to California to pursue a film career. I always felt that I would work here (Los Angeles) until I developed enough of a reputation to be useful on the road and on Broadway. "

Leonard enrolled in classes at the Pasadena Playhouse, where he stood out among the other students, who consisted primarily of bored ex-GIs taking classes paid for by the government. Leonard was not only genuinely interested in acting; he also raised the six hundred dollar tuition himself, and paid his own rent at a small local boarding house, after he could no longer afford the six dollars a week rent at the local YMCA. He was, however, disappointed with the Pasadena Playhouse; he had hoped for a creative experience, but was only confronted with its flat, academic stance. Driven, as always, to act, he soon made his first West Coast stage appearance in a production of Marlowe's "Doctor Faustus." His Boston accent took some getting rid of, of course, but he soon found some work in films and TV. Some of this merely involved working as an usher, for sixty five cents an hour, at the Santa Anita theater in Arcadia; he saw Broderick Crawford in *All The King's Men* at least thirty times. He also worked at an ice cream parlor on Sunset Strip. Walking home late at night, in jeans and a T-shirt, he was often questioned by police, until they got used to his presence and realized he wasn't any sort of criminal.

Nimoy, alongside Lane Bradford, plays his
first extraterrestrial in ZOMBIES OF THE STRATOSPHERE

A very young Leonard Nimoy

Leonard tried constantly to get into films, but his strenuous efforts seemed to be of no avail. "At first," he recalled years later, "like any other teenager anxious to be an actor, I assumed that if I could get into a studio, if I could read a script, I'd get a part. I didn't think I was good-looking enough, but I believed I had enough talent. What I didn't recognize was how terribly competitive the acting field is. There are many people here with a lot of talent. I didn't see that mine was raw and undeveloped. I had to build a background of credits to qualify, had to prepare more meticulously than I'd counted on. "

His friend, actress Ruth Roman, tried to get him involved in a film she was in with Gary Cooper, the Western *Dallas* (1950), in a role which might have been perfect for him, as the character was actually from Boston. His agent got him an interview with the people making the picture, and they promised him a screen test (good news even if he didn't get the part), but this soon degenerated into a classic Hollywood runaround; the role went to someone else, and the screen test never came through. Leonard, inspired by a scene in a movie he'd once seen, went to the producer's office and refused to budge until he saw him— until the producer threatened to call the police. Obviously, real life didn't always work like it did in the movies, and Leonard took the hint and went back to his apartment.

Leonard finally made his own film debut with a brief appearance in the film *Queen For A Day* (1951). He was, however, the title character in the low-budget boxing picture, *Kid Monk Baroni* (1952). In payment, he received 350 dollars and three fifty-dollar suits. Because he was only twenty, he needed court approval for his ten-picture deal with Jack Broder Productions, a contract that provided him with two hundred dollars a week and a twenty-five dollar raise every second picture. *Variety* credited Nimoy with doing a good job despite the hackneyed material he had to work with. This did not propel him into the limelight, but being cast as the lead in any picture—even as obscure an opus as *Baroni*—did wonders for Leonard's confidence. It was to be the only movie he made for Jack Broder's company.

As the lead in *Kid Monk Baroni,* Nimoy was required to have his appearance altered through make-up. Later Leonard recalled, "I was not a thoroughly trained actor, but instinctively my emotions began to respond to my new appearance. I could begin to identify with the internal life of this face—the insecurities, the retiring shyness, the bursts of anger, the paranoia. I found a home behind that make-up. I was much more confident and comfortable than I would have been had I been told to play a handsome young man. Even in *Kid Monk Baroni* I was playing a character outside of the social mainstream—separate, unequal, and alien. I had been raised in a neighborhood rich in Italian culture. Most of my early friends were Italians. Being Jewish I always sensed some element of difference, of separation. Our friendships stopped abruptly at the door of the church. "

Leonard by no means glorifies the picture. In 1970, he told *TV Guide, "Kid Monk Baroni* was the kind of production that takes stars and makes unknowns out of them." Although playing the title role, he was the fifth billed actor in the production. His co-stars included Bruce Cabot, a minor star of the '30s and '40s who had seen better days, and Jack Larson, who was then already well known in the role of Jimmy Olsen on TV's *Superman.*

Leonard also appeared in a variety of lesser motion picture roles at about the same time. He was the Alien zombie (actually a Martian; why the film called them "zombies" was never stated) Narab in the Republic serial *Zombies of the Stratosphere* (1952), his first alien role. He actually has a number of lines in the film and, in the climax, crawls from his wrecked spacecraft to reveal to the hero that a nuclear device is set to go off which will destroy the earth. The serial has had something of a revival in recent years, particularly since it has been Colorimaged by Republic Pictures and made available in syndication in a version edited to play in a two-hour television time slot. The only criticism of the Colorimaging of *Zombies Of The Stratosphere* was the unfortunate decision to make the aliens mint green!

The rest of Leonard's work in the early Fifties was in supporting roles. He was a baseball player in *Rhubarb* (1951); an Indian in *Old Overland Trail* (1953); and a soldier (with one line) in *Them* (1954).

A Pasadena Playhouse production of "Stalag 17" brought Leonard back into contact with his former director from Boston, Boris Sagal. His ability to speak Yiddish made him a shoo-in whenever the touring Yiddish-language theater came into town and needed actors. In 1953, while performing in the Sholem Aleichem play "It's Hard To Be A Jew," he met actress Sandi Zober; they were married in 1954. The draft caught up with him soon afterward.

An eighteen-month stint in the Army took the Nimoys to Atlanta, Georgia in 1955, where he was stationed at Fort McPhearson. There he was assigned to Special Services to write, narrate and emcee GI shows. This didn't stop Leonard from keeping his hand in the acting game outside of his military duties. In his spare time he worked with the Atlanta Theatre Guild where he directed and played the role of Stanley Kowalski in a production of "A Streetcar Named Desire," the only time Sandi Zober ever performed on stage with him. In Army productions Leonard was involved in a variety show featuring Ken Berry, who would go on to star in *F Troop* and *Mayberry RFD*.

The Nimoys' first child, daughter Julie, was born in Atlanta in 1955. Soon after Leonard mustered out and moved his family back to Los Angeles, where they were joined by a new child, son Adam, born in 1956. To support his wife and children, he worked a wide variety of jobs, delivering newspapers, ushering in a movie theater, working in a pet shop and driving a taxi at night. Once, while driving his cab, he picked up a fare named Kennedy at the Bel Air hotel. The young politician from Massachusetts was not nationally known at the time, but Leonard, as a transplanted Bostonian, knew who he was. They had a brief talk about their home state. When they reached the Beverly Hilton, JFK realized he didn't have any cash on him, so Leonard followed him around until he borrowed three dollars for the hard-working cabbie. Since the fare was only a $1.25, the tip was quite generous.

3

A Working Actor

In 1958, Leonard landed a small role in *The Brain Eaters,* the same year that saw the release of *Satan's Satellite's,* the feature version of *Zombies of the Stratosphere.* By this time Leonard was working more and more in episodic television. Parts often came his way as a contract player for ZIV Productions, a company which created plenty of long-forgotten syndicated program fodder in the Fifties and Sixties, as well as *Highway Patrol* and their biggest success, *Sea Hunt.* As a member of ZIV's regular stock company, Leonard usually had some TV work with them every few weeks, at union scale—fifty-five dollars a day, later going as high as eighty a day. Of that association, he recalled, "I began doing more television work, for ZIV. I played stone-cold heavies. I did them in a cliched manner. I am ashamed of those jobs. I earned four, five, six thousand a year, maybe $3,000 as an actor, the rest on other jobs." Those other jobs included working as an usher, soda jerk, vacuum salesman and servicing tropical fish tanks in doctors' offices.

Perhaps the greatest benefit of his association with ZIV was the increased exposure it gave him, which led to roles on many shows by a number of other producers. Ironically, ZIV declined to utilize Leonard's talents in their 1959 series *Men Into Space.* "You're not a space type," they told him, not realizing how far off the mark they truly were.

A good deal of his occasional television roles during this period were villainous: in a 1957 episode of *Highway Patrol,* he played a mob goon who specialized in beating up people. A later episode of that same program ("Hot Dust," 1958) featured him as a young factory worker who flees when he is exposed to a substance he believes has made him a radioactive hazard to other people. Needless to say, Broderick Crawford saves the day. This was not typical casting for Leonard, as he usually played heavies, not sensitive characters, in his early TV appearances. In a 1968 interview with Digby Diehl, Leonard recalled these antisocial roles with some wryness: "I learned how to use a switchblade and a gun, how to kick people, hit people, choke 'em, threaten 'em, torture 'em— all the nice things heavies do."

Still, the roles got better and the work more frequent. Leonard actually appeared on Sea Hunt at least five times as different characters. He was on *Perry Mason,* too— and yes, *he* did it. He even had a small role in a *Twilight Zone* episode: "A Quality of Mercy," with Dean Stockwell. Even *The Outer Limits* made use of his talents on two occasions; one in a small supporting role, the other in a larger guest-starring role. And as long as Western dramas were a staple of television, Leonard appeared in his share of those, including *Gunsmoke, Wagon Train, Rawhide* and *Bonanza.*

In fact, Westerns provided Leonard with some of his best television roles. In one *Wagon Train* episode, first aired October 21, 1959, he played Bernabe Zamora, one of a trio of Mexican brothers who have started a sheep ranch. For this role, Leonard brought the young man's sense of tormented guilt to vivid life.

Another episode of the same series, broadcast the following year, cast Leonard in the smaller but equally pivotal role of a drunken Indian scout. Unfortunately, most Indian roles tended to be stereotyped at the time. For example, in a 1965 episode of *Death Valley Days* ("The Journey"), Leonard played Yellow Eagle, an Indian who wanted to escape from the Cavalry troops escorting him and his people to a new reservation—only to be killed by his own people, who have decided to passively accept the course of history. In other words, Leonard's Yellow Eagle was a "bad" Indian.

The Tall Man was a short-lived series (1960-62) about Deputy Sheriff Pat Garrett (Barry Sullivan) and his troublesome friend Billy "The Kid" Bonney (Clu Galager). The series led Bonney deeper and deeper into crime, but never reached the final, fatal confrontation between the two men. An early episode, "A Bounty For Billy," was scripted by future *Star Trek* writer D.C. Fontana, who had previously been the production secretary for the series. Leonard was cast as Deputy Johnny Swift, an impetuous young lawman. Producer Samuel A. Peeples was so impressed by his approach to the character that he brought Leonard back in the same role in a 1961 episode he scripted, "A Gun Is For Killing." This was the closest Leonard came to a continuing television role until 1966.

In an episode of *The Virginian,* "Man of Violence" (December 25, 1963), Leonard plays Wismer, a man who is tracked down after he robs and kills an old friend of series regular Trampas (Doug McClure). DeForest Kelley plays Lt. Belden, the medic treating Wismer who falsely comes to believe he is responsible for his death.

Leonard's finally received a sympathetic role in a *Dr. Kildare* episode directed by his past mentor from Boston, Elliot Silverstein. The 1963 episode ("An Island Like a Peacock") gave him a rare opportunity to play a more complex character than usual, a sensitive young man in love with a blind girl. Speaking of his actor, award-winning director Silverstein said, "Nimoy is one of the most patient actors I've met. He's remained gentle and dignified throughout, even when he wasn't welcome as a first-line talent as he is today. He has a gentleness and sweetness of disposition that always seeps through. He's probably one of the best trained actors around, with a steadiness of purpose which results in his being able to bear the various degrees of recognition heaped on actors through their careers. He's grown as a man and therefore as an actor, rather than the reverse."

Gene Roddenberry saw this episode and was impressed by the performance, but didn't realize he was hiring the same actor when he cast Leonard in a guest role in his Marine Corps drama, *The Lieutenant,* in 1964. *The Lieutenant,* a series about the peacetime Marine corps, starred Gary Lockwood as Lt. William Rice. In the episode with Leonard, "The Highest Tradition," Rice is assigned to write a history of his platoon, which was wiped out—except for one survivor— in World War Two. The survivor, Lt. Booney, is regarded as a hero, but he mistakenly believes himself a coward, since he was not with the platoon when the Nazis destroyed it. Leonard appears as Greg Sanders, a flashy, eccentric Hollywood actor/director who wants to film Lt. Booney's story but insists on making dramatic changes. Lt. Rice has to deal with both these men, and Booney finally accepts that he did all he could by trying to rejoin his platoon. This was an interesting role for Leonard, as most of his characters tended to be introspective; as Sanders, he was playing against type. This performance made a profound impression on producer Roddenberry. (Roddenberry's future wife, Majel Barrett, also appeared in this episode.)

Roddenberry was already working on a new, proposed series and planned to employ Leonard in an important role. It would be a while before the project got off the ground. *Star Trek* was a hard sell to the networks, as Roddenberry envisioned using the series as a platform from which to address current issues, which television frequently shied away from.

Leonard studied for a time with actor Jeff Corey, taking part in a weekly, twenty-student session, until 1960, when Corey asked him to become a teacher at his studio. Leonard's initial return to class was prompted by the influx, in the late 1950s, of New York actors into Hollywood. "At the time," he later told Digby Diehl in 1968, " I was a reliable actor, the kind who knew his lines and didn't bump into the other actors. And I joined the sour grapes chorus when those guys came in from New York and started taking all the jobs, until I began to realize that they were bringing to film acting something we hadn't seen in a long while. Along with all the mumbling, scratching and lint-picking, there was a special kind of nitty-gritty excitement that actors like Brando, and Tony Franciosa, and Montgomery Clift were putting in their work. I suddenly realized that I couldn't really act. And that was tough to admit, since I'd been taking money for acting for quite a while."

Studying with Corey was a revelation. "Well, I was absolutely fascinated: he started talking about 'subtext' and 'dramatic theme' and 'character ambivalence' and I knew this was it," Leonard continued. "I began to see how guys like Brando made their work so exciting, and within three weeks my own acting improved notably, because I was adding awareness to the technique I had already accumulated."

At first, he was nonplussed working with other students, many of whom were amateurs, and friction developed between him and Corey. Leonard almost dropped out but decided, despite a serious cold, to go back, as he felt that if he didn't show, Corey would think he had backed down! So Leonard went to the second class despite his illness, and what had been, to him, an argument with Corey, somehow turned into a dialogue, and ultimately a true friendship.

Through his classes at Corey's studio, Leonard met actor Vic Morrow (*The Blackboard Jungle*), who would eventually star in the popular series *Combat!* Morrow was directing a stage production of Jean Genet's *Deathwatch*, and cast him as the prisoner LeFranc. Leonard's reviews were good, and he joined Morrow in the film version soon after. He co-produced the movie with Vic Morrow, while Morrow directed. Made independently for $125,000, it premiered on January 20, 1965 at The Movie Theatre in San Francisco. Unable to find a distributor, they attempted limited distribution on their own, but the film only played college campuses where the work of Jean Genet was popular. Leonard and Paul Mazursky played the leads and the film's technical crew included cinematographer Haskell Wexler and film editor Verna Fields.

Leonard also appeared in another movie adaptation of Genet's work, *The Balcony*, with Shelley Winters and Peter Falk. In his interview with Diehl in 1968, Leonard said, "Genet gets under your skin. You become so involved with the texture and ideas in his writing that it envelops you. After a while, you have to do it as a catharsis. It's marvelous actor material because it's all subtext. We had experiences performing *Deathwatch* that were frightening. Some nights the play would completely take over, and we would have emotional moments of laughing or crying that we couldn't control. The audiences sometimes didn't know what was happening, but the emotional charge was fantastic."

In 1962, Leonard opened his own acting studio, which he operated until 1965. His students included Richard Chamberlain, who was cast as Dr. Kildare while studying with him. Pat Boone studied with Leonard when he decided to tackle "West Side Story" on stage, and other musicians followed suit. Teen idol Fabian Forte took classes, and did interesting work for television, even though his career never soared as a thespian. Trumpeter Herb Alpert was another protegé in whom Leonard saw great talent, but that never reached the general public, and Alpert remained best known for "Tijuana Taxi" and other hits, not as an actor.

In *I Am Not Spock,* Leonard revealed that his approach to teaching was heavily influenced by Stanislavski. He wrote, "I am very much affected by the clothes I wear. Putting on a cape can make me feel quite dashing and romantic. An old work jacket, work boots, and an old dirty cap can make me feel quite seedy. The character's clothes begin to affect me inwardly, as does the make-up. There are various other elements which lead me to the core of the character. But the externals are very helpful."

He drew great satisfaction from his work as an acting teacher and coach, and his many students, regardless of their later careers, remember him with fondness. It was with regret that Leonard closed his studio, a mere two weeks before beginning work on the show that would make him a household name.

A Shot at the Stars

By the time the single season of MGM's *The Lieutenant* went off the air, Gene Roddenberry had submitted a proposed *Star Trek* format to them. The basic premise is now familiar to millions, but the characters were different. The Captain was Robert T. April, his executive officer the logical female "Number One," and the navigator José Tyler. The ship's doctor was nicknamed "Bones," but was otherwise a completely different character. Mr. Spock was in the proposal, but described as possessing "a red-hued satanic look" and, according to one source, absorbing energy through a red plate in his navel! The Enterprise and its mission made it to the screen unchanged. Roddenberry insisted the science fiction be logical, presenting the story with the same techniques used in other drama, without falling on convenient fantasy resolutions with no basis reality.

MGM said they were interested, but not at the present time. Other studios followed suit, providing Roddenberry with a file full of politely worded brush-offs. A shift in the prevailing winds occurred when Desilu Studios was looking for new series ideas. Desilu, the studio behind *I Love Lucy* and Lucille Ball's other television programs, was hurting financially; *Lucy* was their only viable property, and they frequently rented out their facilities to other studios. Desilu was impressed with Roddenberry and his ideas, including *Star Trek*. They took a chance and signed him to a three-year pilot development deal. Roddenberry pitched *Star Trek* to CBS's highest ranking network executives. They listened intently for two hours, and he emerged convinced he'd sold them.

They were certainly interested in his thoughts on saving costs and designing ships, but their questions had another motive entirely. When he was finished, they thanked him politely, but passed on the proposal. They already had a science fiction series of their own in the works. It seems Roddenberry may have inadvertently helped them launch *Lost In Space,* which even, by some coincidence, had the Robinson family embarking on a five-year mission of exploration. *Lost In Space* premiered in 1965, and, like *Star Trek,* ran for three seasons.

Roddenberry, despite disenchantment with CBS' cavalier treatment, kept on trying. In May of 1964, NBC offered $20,000 in story development money; Roddenberry would develop three story ideas for a *Star Trek* pilot, then write a script based on the idea chosen by the network. They picked "The Cage" and Roddenberry set to work on a shooting script. In September of 1964, the script was approved; the first *Star Trek* episode received the green light.

Roddenberry remembered his commitment to Leonard and arranged a meeting. The actor assumed he would be trying out for the part of Spock and never realized he was already Roddenberry's preferred choice. The prospect of a regular series was exciting to Leonard, who, despite his frequent guest appearances on television, didn't have a stable income. He had some misgivings; if the show was an unmitigated flop would he become a laughingstock, forever derided for wearing those silly-looking pointed ears? In conference with his friend Vic Morrow, he even pondered developing make-up that would completely conceal his face. Fortunately he thought better of this idea.

"The Cage" began shooting with a cast of characters drawn from the original format, although the captain was now named Christopher Pike. Pike was portrayed by Jeffrey Hunter, who had the rare distinction of having played Jesus Christ (in the 1961 religious epic, *King of Kings).* John Hoyt played the ship's doctor, Philip Boyce. Leonard essayed the role of Spock, but the Vulcan's trademark logic still belonged to Number One, the character portrayed by Majel Barrett. Spock's red skin was dropped because the majority of television sets in American homes in the mid-Sixties still only showed black-and-white; red appeared nearly black on these screens, far too dark and light-absorbing for the actor to get anything subtle across. A nearly normal skin tone with a faint yellowish-green tinge was decided upon. Unfortunately, he looked downright green on some color televisions, but this was due to color mixing at local stations and not intended by the creators.

Spock occupied a background role. This didn't bother him too much; whatever else happened, the pilot provided him with three consecutive weeks of work, the longest single job he'd ever had in television to that date. As the basic concept of Spock was still in the embryonic stages, his reactions were far from logical. When Spock and the somewhat grim-tempered Captain Pike discovered an alien plant with blue leaves that emitted eerie, harmonic tones, it was Spock who smiled at the phenomenon with an almost childlike innocence and wonder. The initial concept of the character included a fascination with all things alien, but that fascination was not yet tempered with the rigors of Vulcan logic. For the rest of the story, Spock stood by while his superior officer, Number One, took most of the initiative in the Captain's absence. Captain Pike, needless to say, had fallen into the clutches of aliens, and was in the midst of making some serious points about the dangers of preferring comfortable illusions to the risks and opportunities offered by reality.

NBC liked the pilot. It surpassed anything done in the genre for television before, and looked better than most science fiction films. No one had a bad word to say about the finished product. Everyone at NBC thought *Star Trek* was great. They rejected it It was *too* intelligent; NBC feared the story would go over the heads of the television audience. If *Star Trek* was only a bit more action-oriented, they mused, it would appeal to a wider audience. In an unprecedented move, the network gave Roddenberry the go-ahead to produce a *second* pilot.

They also wanted to get rid of the guy with the pointed ears. They didn't understand him at all, and besides, there was always the slim but unpleasant possibility that religious groups might be offended by such a sinister, demonic looking character.

Roddenberry, undeterred, set out to revamp the show, but was determined to keep Spock. An alien presence on the ship was, to him, a vital part of *Star Trek*. He discarded Number One, who, as a woman in a command position, the network executives liked even less than the Vulcan. In place of Number One, Roddenberry promoted Spock, bringing him closer to the forefront. Leonard had all but forgotten *Star Trek,* and his contract had expired, but Roddenberry got Leonard back on his pet project.

This time NBC wanted three complete scripts. All three ("Mudd's Women" by Stephen Kandel, "Omega Glory" by Roddenberry, and "Where No Man Has Gone Before" by Samuel A. Peeples) had plenty of action. The network chose the Peeples script. By this time, Jeffrey Hunter was no longer available; the ship's captain was renamed James T. Kirk, and talented Canadian actor William Shatner was cast. Leonard had worked with Shatner once before, in a 1964 episode of *The Man From Uncle*, "The Project Strigas Affair" in which Leonard played a Russian.

Roddenberry worked out a few kinks in Spock, giving him an expanded background as well as the cool logic previously attributed to Number One. With the revamped Vulcan, and a more flexible captain, the second *Star Trek* pilot won approval from the executives at NBC. *Star Trek* would become a regular series.

Roddenberry and crew geared up for full-time production. A new ship's doctor was added in the person of Leonard "Bones" McCoy, portrayed by DeForest Kelley, who had previously worked with Leonard in an episode of *The Virginian*. This would prove a very important addition to the show; the chemistry between the three leads— particularly between the cold, impervious Vulcan and the volatile, compassionate Earth doctor— would play a major role in the program's success.

One obstacle remained: the make-up department had yet to come up with a painless means of applying the Spock ears. The ears were irritating and painful where the glue was applied, one reason for Spock's stiffness since facial movement, however slight, compounded the discomfort. Matters were confounded by contractual obligations as the ears had to be made by the props department, not the make-up department. Considerable variations in the shape of the ears (as well as in Spock's general appearance) can be seen in the two pilots. Leonard was frustrated, and expressed his dissatisfaction to his producer. Roddenberry could tell his anguish was real—but what could he do? Finally, grasping at straws, he promised the actor that if, after thirteen episodes, Leonard was still unhappy with the ears, he would personally write them out of the series. When the actor thought about it and broke into laughter, the fate of the ears was sealed—and Spock still has them to this day.

Star Trek debuted on September 8, 1966. The first episode was "Man Trap" even though "Where No Man Has Gone Before" was filmed first; it aired third. Thus, McCoy was in the debut episode despite having been added later The fourth episode, "The Naked Time," featured insights into Spock's mixed planetary heritage. Its plot, concerning a dehibilitating disease, gave Leonard the chance to play a scene in which Spock wept openly over his inability to express his love for his human mother. The tension between Spock's human side and his more dominant Vulcan half made the character intriguing. Everyone wants to keep control of their emotions; Spock stood out as a character who had them virtually licked, but was still capable of feeling them. There was humanity behind the computer-like facade.

In the June 1968 issue of *Variety,* Leonard wrote, "During the first season of *Star Trek* a wise director gave me this advice: 'Build in all the character elements you can find right now while you still have your strength. As time goes on, the attrition will be devastating. ' I took his advice and am very grateful for it. The fact is, a great deal of talent is required to work successfully in television—perhaps even more than in features. The finished TV product is nothing more than a series of educated, artistic guesses determined solely by the previous experience of the individuals involved. Time to cogitate, to digest or to live with an idea before committing it to film is strictly forbidden. The very basic form of creativity is undermined. If you'll forgive a tongue-twisting axiom, 'Thesis versus antithesis results in dramatic synthesis. Time and creative energy provide the dramatic content. ' Remove the element of time and the synthesis becomes forced and arbitrary, lacking fresh insight." Leonard went on to reveal that, "On the *Star Trek* set we've actually had rewrites arrive seconds and even minutes after the scene had been shot. Time beats TV by a nose. And the viewers finish out of the money!"

Leonard continued to do his best to rise to the challenges of the medium. Unbeknownst to him, viewers would raise his character to a status equal to the show's ostensible star, William Shatner.

In "Dagger Of The Mind," Leonard first applied the Vulcan mind meld, which demonstrated that Spock was still, in his logical fashion, capable of deep empathy.

Leonard came to the forefront in "The Galileo Seven." Spock was stranded on a dangerous world with McCoy, Scotty and four other crewmen; his decisions are hampered by the doubts of McCoy and the others, but his logic prevails. The conflict between his two sides came to the forefront again in "This Side of Paradise." Here, Leonard portrays a Spock in love when an alien spore releases his emotions from logic-imposed bondage. In "Devil In The Dark," the mind-meld came into use again; in Harlan Ellison's "City On The Edge Of Forever," Spock is faced with a world full of illogical humans, as he and Kirk travel through time to keep McCoy from altering historical events on 20th Century Earth. Slowly Spock became as important as Kirk.

Shatner even reminded some series scriptwriters that *he* was the Captain and later acknowledged friction between himself and Leonard, but indicated it was a matter of the past. He said, "We went through that fire together and today we are fast friends.

Leonard is an honest man and a fine craftsman." At the time Shatner was so concerned he counted his lines in each new script. Norman Spinrad once related the story of the time he visited the set of the episode he had scripted, "The Doomsday Machine," and witnessed the director struggling with a dilemma. He was searching for an alternative way for Leonard to react with Shatner in a scene because keeping a line would have given the Vulcan one too many in Shatner's eyes.

When Leonard was not busy being Spock, he relaxed, as he described in an issue of *TV Star Parade* during the original run of *Star Trek*. He told the magazine, ". . . I enjoy playing the guitar, listening to recordings—I like all kinds of music, prefer the Beatles and the Monkees among the groups and Frank Sinatra and Ray Charles among the individual singers—and catching the newest films; Anthony Quinn is my favorite actor and the actress I admire most is Anne Bancroft. I enjoy TV too, naturally, but I work so late into the evening on *Star Trek* that I rarely have time to watch other shows, and so I have no favorite program.

"The colors I am most partial to are green and blue," he continued, "and I go for tasty food of every description. Woodworking takes a good deal of my free time (it gives me a kick to work with my hands around the house), and tropical fish and photography are two of my other hobbies. I enjoy fishing and haul out my hook-and-line whenever the mood seizes me.

"My ambition: I want to be the best actor I can possibly become, and am working hard to perfect my talents. Eventually, I would like to act in good feature films— in roles which have bite and say something about life," he concluded. He went on to solicit fan letters—and even gave his home address!

When *Star Trek* premiered in September of 1966, many merchandising tie-ins were already in the works, including LEONARD NIMOY PRESENTS MR. SPOCK'S MUSIC FROM OUTER SPACE. Although an unwieldy length for a title, it made clear what the album was, along with the photo of Mr. Spock on the cover. Dot Records had secured all the rights to an album tie-in and even approached Leonard to become involved. Leonard's musician friend Don Henley, bound for greater fame as a member of the popular Eagles and later as a solo performer, handled the business end of his musical career. Dot intended to exploit Leonard's name by having him perform a couple of pieces. (Leonard had not done much singing before this. His only previous professional experience had been in 1965 with Juliet Prowse in a stage production of "Irma La Douce.") While he sang three songs ("Where Is Love," "Lost In The Stars" and "You Are Not Alone"), the rest were recitations with Leonard portraying Spock. These three pieces include "Alien," in which he discusses the Spock character in a dramatic monologue, as if Spock were addressing humankind collectively. There was also "Twinkle, Twinkle Little Earth" and "A Visit To A Sad Planet," the last played as though Spock were recounting an incident in the travels of the Enterprise in which they discover a planet whose civilization had destroyed itself, with the punchline being that the planet had called itself Earth. The remainder of the initial album consisted of instrumentals, including the only commercially available version of the *Star Trek* theme for many years to come, as well as other science fiction type music. Interestingly, the theme from *Mission: Impossible* is included, years before he would join the cast of that series.

The album cover features an early publicity photo which depicts Spock holding a model of the Enterprise, while the back cover is a photo of Leonard Nimoy in civilian garb, perhaps the first time many people saw what he really looked like. Care was taken in the production and arrangement of the melodies and Leonard's recitations demonstrate a fine speaking voice. While his singing has been the object of some ridicule, he's not bad, although his best work appears on later albums. MR. SPOCK'S MUSIC FROM OUTER SPACE sold 130,000 copies and produced a hot single, "Visit To A Sad Planet. " The single, featuring a colorful photo sleeve of Mr. Spock, is now rare, as are all the early albums.

THE TWO SIDES OF LEONARD NIMOY came out a

few months later. The second album is more polished and coherent and even Leonard's singing shows marked improvement and greater self-confidence. The second album took the strengths of the first to produce a package for more than Leonard Nimoy or Spock fans. The songs are folk/rock, fast and yet gentle. The album still capitalized on the *Star Trek* connection; one side offers songs and recitations as done by Mr. Spock while the other offers Leonard as himself, singing what he likes. There are ballads on both sides, one of which describes Mr. Spock's first love and seems inspired by "This Side Of Paradise." To the surprise of many, Leonard did a song based on the fantasy novel *The Hobbit* entitled "The Ballad of Bilbo Baggins." The bouncy novelty tune is continually singled out when his recording career is discussed, whether in such disparate places as the syndicated Dr. Demento radio show or on *Late Night With David Letterman.*

Leonard proved he can sing on his second album. The songs are not just standards, but obscure tunes which deserve recognition. For instance, "Cotton Candy" is an original written by one of the *Star Trek* production crew.

Another selection, "Desiderata," is a recitation of a very literate piece of philosophy written several hundred years ago. It became a top 40 hit in the Seventies recorded by someone else, even though the later version was not as good as Leonard's.

1966 was a good year for Leonard. After years as a guest star, he now had a series of his own; the relief afforded by regular work was quite a boon to him and his family. His yearly income rose from sixteen to 150 thousand dollars in the course of the first season alone. It was, however, still too early for him to suspect just how far the character of Spock would take him.

Leonard Nimoy in a scene from STAR TREK's "Dagger of the Mind"

The Mission Continues

Although it never achieved high Nielsen ratings, *Star Trek* soon amassed a large, loyal following. Writer Harlan Ellison sent a letter to 5,000 science fiction fans asking them to support the show by writing to NBC. This, with its letterhead bearing the names of a "Committee" of top science fiction writers, was responsible for the first *Star Trek* letter campaign.

Spock, largely due to his fascinating otherness, was easily the most popular character on the show. In Boston, one barber shop even featured a photo of Leonard on the wall, with a legend describing the style as "The Spock Haircut" underneath. Proprietor Max Nimoy was all too happy to reveal that Spock was his son. In fact, locals even started calling the elder Nimoy "Mr. Spock" in deference to his role in the creation of the character. Mother Dora frequently found her own work interrupted by teenaged fans who came into her store just to look at Spock's Mom! Even the great science fiction writer and general pundit, Isaac Asimov, was intrigued. In a 1967 *TV Guide* article ("Mr. Spock Is Dreamy," 4/29/67), he pondered the mystery of Mr. Spock's strange appeal, especially to women. Could it be sexual? So it seemed. Perhaps, contrary to what was generally believed, women thought that being smart was sexy. Of course there was the challenge of trying to crack that icy veneer to find the man beneath. One intrigued woman wrote and asked exactly how alien Mr. Spock was, in terms of anatomy. . . the parts of his body that weren't shown on television, that is.

Leonard soon started doing public appearances. In 1966, he and William Shatner were invited to appear in Hollywood's annual Christmas parade. This newfound fame was no guarantee of respect, however, for while the parade announcer got Shatner's name correct, he introduced the other *Star Trek* star as "Leonard Nimsy." Despite this gaffe, Leonard was, for the first time in his life, frequently recognized on the street, and constantly besieged for autographs. He took it all in good humor, although he soon became weary of smart-aleck fans asking him where he'd left his ears.

Fan mail began to pour in, too, a great deal of it from younger viewers. In a 1967 *TV Guide* article, Leonard summed it up neatly: "The kids dig the fact that Spock is cool." Gene Roddenberry, as might be expected, had a more highbrow explanation: "We're all imprisoned within ourselves. We're all aliens on this strange planet. So people find identification with Spock."

This was uncharted territory for Leonard. At first he was determined to answer all his fan mail by himself; thirty or so letters a week was no big deal. Then the numbers began to grow, week by week, until thousands of messages were pouring in. Finally he had to hire an assistant, Teresa Victor, to help him.

Fame gave Leonard a chance to speak out on the issues of the day. In a *TV Star Parade* interview (January 1968), he talked about LSD. He said, "It is a useful tool in the hands of proper medical experts. I am convinced, as a result of reports that I have read, that it will bring about very useful effects in certain instances and under suitable and necessary medical controls. However, as it is being used by so many young people as a means of escape and personal investigation *without* control, I consider it rather dangerous.

He continued, "There have been too many unsettling reports of young people using it without the necessary supervision and having difficulty recuperating from the trip. In many cases, I believe that young people resort to drugs with the excuse that it will help develop their minds, whereas they haven't done the necessary work involved for themselves so that this *could* happen.

"The point is— they are looking for a drug or pill which will do the work for them, and this attitude in life is disastrous whether LSD is involved or not. The drugs can, I understand, be properly used, when the essential mental climate and conditions are already present— however, I believe in natural developmental processes of the mind. The creative process for me has always operated best at the very conscious level— in other words, only when I'm in complete control of my own thinking do I feel that I am creating at my best.

"Satisfaction for me," he said, "the greatest satisfaction has always come from doing a job well as a result of work, time, energy and effort invested properly. I'm not a believer in the existence of magic or any quick, convenient way to get an exciting, creative result. "

There was a down side to his newfound popularity. Early in *Star Trek*'s run, NBC arranged for Leonard to be the Grand Marshall of Medford, Oregon's annual Pear Blossom Festival; his first real promotional trip. He was unprepared for the chaos. The parade went without a hitch—but it had been announced he would sign autographs in a small park at the end of the parade route. A crowd, with a large number of young people, actually followed Leonard. By the time he reached the park, it was swarming with large crowds of people. The lone park employee was swamped by this madness; traffic was completely fouled up. In the end, Medford police had to "rescue" Leonard from his fans.

Eventually people turned down the chance for a Spock/ Nimoy appearance. Macy's, the famous New York department store, declined to have Leonard appear to promote one of his record albums. They honestly admitted they couldn't handle the crowds. Leonard turned down many requests for public appearances because they asked him to wear the ears; he estimated losing about fifty thousand dollars by passing up these offers.

His popularity manifested itself in a bewildering variety of ways. Spock was the only *Star Trek* character to merit solo reproduction as a model kit. While Kirk and Sulu joined him as small figures in AMT's Enterprise Bridge model, a larger diorama kit pitted a six-inch Spock against a three-headed alien serpent. In 1975, Spock and other *Star Trek* characters would have the dubious honor of being reproduced as popsicle molds!

Leonard/Spock's face also appeared on a variety of toy packages, including Sixties-vintage phaser rifles and the ever-popular *Star Trek* disc gun. "I Grok Spock" buttons, referring to Robert A. Heinlein's 1961 novel *Stranger In A Strange Land,* began to crop up as well. By this point, the NBC executives who had wanted to give Spock the axe were acting as if they'd been for the character all along. Leonard's place in the public consciousness was rock solid.

In 1967, Leonard's earlier film, *Deathwatch,* received a wider release, perhaps inspired by his increased visibility. The actor worried that his younger fans might be put off by the film's "Mature" rating.

Mostly Leonard worked on *Star Trek.* While the series was in actual production, it was a full-time job—and more. He arrived at the studio at 6:30 in the morning, five days a week, just to get into his make-up. Complications were avoided; he simply wore his hair in the Spock cut (it is not known if Max the barber ever actually had any customers request that particular look) most of the time. He usually wore horn-rimmed glasses during his off-hours as his eyebrows needed to be partially shaved off to make way for the famous arched eyebrows. The working day usually lasted at least twelve hours—but quite often ran even longer. Leonard frequently rode a bicycle around the studio lot when he wasn't involved in shooting. This proved a sensible means of getting around, and other cast members followed suit.

The actors were better off financially than they had ever been. Leonard upgraded his personal transportation, replacing his battered old car with a new Buick luxury car; Shatner went for something sportier; DeForest Kelley bought a Thunderbird—which he managed to ram into Leonard's Buick one day at the end of shooting. Things proceeded amicably, but passers-by were nonplussed to see a normal-looking man exchanging insurance information with a Vulcan in full regalia.

By the time the second season of *Star Trek* began, Spock had become a pivotal character. The first episode of the season

("Amok Time," written by Theodore Sturgeon; September 15, 1967) took *Star Trek* viewers to Spock's home world, Vulcan, in a fascinating look at that planet's society and culture. An underlying sexual tension was exploited as Spock began to act irrationally; it was time for his mating cycle. Leonard invented the Vulcan hand signal to accompany the greeting: "Live long and prosper. " At the time, he stated, "I decided that the Vulcans were a 'hand-oriented' people. They touch index fingers and they have a greeting which says, 'Live Long And Prosper.'"

The gesture—with both hands touching—came from a Jewish blessing delivered by rabbis to their congregation. The congregation was not supposed to see the gesture—but Leonard, as a boy, couldn't resist the temptation to peek. And so, this gesture, which represents the Hebrew letter "Shin," the first letter in the word "Shaddai" (a reference to the Almighty), became forever associated with the fictional Vulcan culture. Leonard explained this a decade later by revealing, "The secret is that Mr. Spock is Jewish. "

This was not frivolous. Leonard's religious upbringing provides him with a strong moral and ethical background; he overcame his initial doubts about donning the pointed ears of Vulcan when he realized the character of Spock would provide him with a platform to express his personal views. Leonard told the August 25, 1968 *New York Times,* "Now I haven't been able to work these ideas into every script, but this is the kind of thing I'm working for. *Star Trek* is a cut above the average dramatic series generally, but we still have our share of clunkers. Perhaps I get a really good opportunity to bring out Spock in one of every six." Indeed, another aspect of the character's appeal is his unassailable integrity, a trait which derives from Leonard himself. Unfortunately, *Star Trek's* third season would prove to be a tribulation for both the actor and his character.

6 Stumbling Through Space

The third season of *Star Trek* almost never happened. It took an almost unprecedented outpouring of fan mail, organized by Bjo Trimble, to convince NBC to rescind its cancellation. The network even announced its decision to keep the show on the air, late in the second season, in order to allay the fears of their audience.

Leonard, meanwhile, spent his time off from the show doing theatre. During the spring of 1968, he starred in Gore Vidal's comedy, "Visit To A Small Planet" at the Pheasant Run Playhouse in Chicago. His role as an alien who visits Earth must have had particular impact in light of the fact that he was also appearing on television every week as Mr. Spock. The *Chicago Daily News* kicked off a trend that was to dog Leonard's stage reviews, no matter how positive, for years to come; their review was headlined: "Big Ears Bring Big Fame To Star Of Star Trek."

Leonard also became involved in the growing peace movement. On one occasion, he met Dr. Benjamin Spock, who was then awaiting trial. The famous doctor's response upon meeting his television namesake (the Vulcan's name was a complete coincidence) was immediate: "Have you been indicted yet?"

In the meantime, NBC was sneakily shifting its stance toward *Star Trek*. They announced that the show would air in a 7:30 PM, prime time slot on Mondays. . . only to turn around and stick *Star Trek* on at 10:00 PM on Friday. The time slot reeked with the stench of certain death; *Rowan and Martin's Laugh-In* had a prior

Leonard
Nimoy
in "Plato's
Stepchildren"
from the
third, and
last, season
of STAR TREK

claim. They only contracted for thirteen episodes instead of a full season. Ultimately, the series did ran a full season one last time.

Gene Roddenberry was justifiably incensed, and withdrew as the show's producer. He originally brought in Gene L. Coon as his replacement, but Coon had health problems, as well as other commitments. Roddenberry was then forced to bring in people he didn't know. They came highly recommended, but had their own ideas—which is to say they knew nothing at all about *Star Trek*. The third season contained a remarkably high percentage of bad shows. . . more than could be explained by the program's unfortunate growing reliance on formulaic plots. The character who suffered most was Spock.

Leonard once again played a focal role in a season opener. Unfortunately, this time the season began with what is regarded, by many, as *Star Trek*'s worst episode: "Spock's Brain" (9/20/ 68). Spock's brain is stolen by gorgeous women who need it to power their computer in another "descendants of a technologically advanced people who don't know how to keep things running" plot. This leaves Spock with little to do beyond stumbling around, zombie-like, with a clamp-like medical device attached to his head. Leonard had *some* lines, however; for no logical reason, the computer speaks with his voice. Perhaps his vocal cords were stolen as well—but this is never mentioned in the story. *Star Trek* had taken a nose-dive into low comedy.

Leonard was unhappy. When Roddenberry was in charge, he had enjoyed an exchange of ideas with the show's producers, but now his words fell on deaf ears. The very next episode, "The Enterprise Incident," is a case in point. Although the original story by D. C. Fontana was more intelligent than "Spock's Brain," it was marred by other hands. Fontana bore the brunt of fan disapproval for this one until the truth of the rewrite was revealed. Spock romances a female Romulan commander in a most un-Vulcan manner—and lies (the notorious "Vulcan Death Grip" ruse), something he is supposed to be incapable of doing.

The producers were oblivious to protests. When Leonard attempted to suggest changes to make another script (the awkward and embarrassing "Spectre of the Gun," 10/25/68) more logical, no one listened. His memos to the producers became more and more exasperated. Near the end, they were simply criticisms. He felt no qualms pointedly stating that the episode "Whom Gods Destroy" (1/3/69) was a bad remake of the first season episode "Dagger of the Mind." By the time the series went off the air, Leonard was tired of the show. In a 1969 interview, apparently still exasperated by the tribulations of the final season, he summed up his experience saying, "During the show I was in every scene with William Shatner and was required to follow him, not unlike a faithful dog." A far cry, indeed, from his earlier enthusiasm toward *Star Trek*.

During *Star Trek*'s descent into apparent oblivion, Leonard recorded albums. His third, THE WAY I FEEL, dispensed with both the Mr. Spock/*Star Trek* tie-in and folk rock instead venturing into Country Western. Only two of the songs stand out as memorable. "Where It's At," a musical philosophical recitation, and "Here We Go Round Again," a rousing call for brotherhood, come closest in keeping with the folk/rock sounds of the second album.

The fourth album, THE TOUCH OF LEONARD NIMOY, is disappointing. Only "Maiden Wine" (which he had sung in the *Star Trek* episode "Plato's Stepchildren") is interesting and even that isn't up to the quality of the earlier albums.

Leonard's fifth and final excursion into the realm of song, THE NEW WORLDS OF LEONARD NIMOY, was released after *Star Trek* had been cancelled in 1969 and he had gone on to join the cast of *Mission: Impossible*. If the fourth album was disappointing, this last was more so. Absolutely none of the selections are memorable. No more albums followed. Leonard's creative energies had turned to other areas. It should be noted that while it was common in the Sixties and Seventies for television stars to release record albums, most never released more than one. Even Telly Savalas had an album out, but no one sustained a series of albums as Leonard did with his five. He would later do other albums purely of the spoken word, but these were completely different from the five Dot Records released.

7 Gone to Earth

When *Star Trek* went off the air, Leonard found himself in a bureaucratic hassle. At first glance, it almost seemed reasonable. Since *Star Trek* was going off the air, the studio requested he vacate his office on the Paramount lot. He agreed to have all his personal belongings out of the office in a few weeks. Unfortunately, this wasn't good enough. A new writer for the popular *Mission: Impossible* needed the space— immediately. Leonard and Teresa Victor stored their furnishings and supplies in her apartment on insultingly short notice. Meanwhile, he had no work. This need would be filled in ironic fashion in light of Paramount's cavalier treatment.

Mission: Impossible had a history the opposite of *Star Trek*. The show premiered in 1966, and received little public response—but its popularity grew. Its opening sequences, with the famous self-destructing tape recorder, set the tone for the missions that followed. The adventures always hinged on elaborate deception of enemy agents and other villains, through complicated use of disinformation, high technology and remarkable disguises. Somehow, in the world of *Mission: Impossible,* a simple rubber mask would provide an impenetrable disguise. Usually a second actor portrayed the disguised character and when the time came for revelation, the actor would reach up to pull off their mask— and the camera would cut to the first actor peeling off the disguise! However unrealistic and implausible, the show was wildly entertaining, and soon became a hit.

Leonard
Nimoy in
MISSION
IMPOSSIBLE

In the original line-up of *Mission: Impossible,* actor Martin Landau played the master of disguise, Rollin Hand. In 1969, Landau and his wife Barbara Bain (who played agent Cinnamon Carter) left the show when they couldn't negotiate a contract to their satisfaction. The studio, faced with a major gap in the cast, contacted Leonard's agent.

Leonard was intrigued; the seven thousand dollars he received for each episode didn't hurt, either. His intended character would be a replacement for Martin Landau's chameleon, and would give him the opportunity to play a different role— perhaps several—each week. Paramount signed him to an eight-script trial run to see if the actor and the program worked well together. A few weeks after his forced departure from Paramount, Leonard once again returned to the studio lot. He knew it all could have been avoided if only the studio hadn't been in such a hurry to get rid of him! But as a studio executive told him, "We love you— now. We just didn't love you *then.* "

It wasn't long before it became apparent Leonard's co-starring stint on the series was going to work. He soon signed a four year contract with CBS and Paramount at the generous sum of seven thousand dollars per episode and joined the *Mission: Impossible* cast full-time as Paris.

Mission: Impossible was easier work than *Star Trek.* The scripts weren't as deep and had little to do with serious issues; there was little ensemble work. Even so, the cast got along well; there was very little pressure as the show was already a major hit. Even the shooting schedule was more relaxed. Leonard had found a comfortable, well-paying job. The show even provided him with tailored suits and sports jackets from the top names in fashion.

About this time, Leonard opened his own pet shop: Leonard Nimoy's Pet Pad, in the San Fernando Valley, where the motto was "Come on in and be petted." He had worked in a pet shop during his early years of Hollywood struggle; now he owned one, and was the boss.

Perhaps the only drawback Leonard encountered in *Mission: Impossible* was his character of Paris. Which is to say that there *was* no character to Paris at all. None worth mentioning, anyway. He was a cipher, a blank slate on which disguises were to be placed as the necessities of the scripts demanded. There was no core personality. True, Paris gave Leonard the opportunity to portray a variety of characters— once. He impersonated a Chinese military officer, a Nazi, a Gypsy and a South American revolutionary leader; a magician, an Arab, a Japanese Kabuki actor, and a Russian; he even played a robot in one episode. In the midst of all this, he never once actually played Paris, the character he'd been signed on to portray. During his second season, some attempt was made to remedy this but the producers remained unwilling to stray very far from the series well-established popular format. After two years of pleasant acting exercises, Leonard thought it was time to move on. He had no complaint with the program; he just wanted to do something different. It took a while to persuade his agent, but an amicable departure was arranged in 1971. In an interview in the July 13, 1973 issue of the *Los Angeles Free Press*, Leonard said, "It became repetitious and I became a zombie, and I asked them to let me out. They were nice enough to agree." His stint on *Mission: Impossible*, close on the heels of *Star Trek,* left him well-to-do. He was now free to return to theatre.

Before returning to the stage, Leonard took part in two movie projects, *Assault On the Wayne* (a TV movie) and the theatrically released Western, *Catlow*, both filmed in the early part of 1971.

Assault On The Wayne is a fairly average thriller made for television. Had it been made for theatrical release it would have had more violence and harsher language, but would have essentially told the same story. The directing is lackluster as it looks like any number of other films and TV shows set aboard a submarine. The director never uses the camera to show what life aboard a submerged sub is like, such as was done a few years later by Wolfgang Peterson in *Das Boot*, the film about life aboard a German U-boat in the second World War.

Leonard and Lloyd Haynes had previously worked together in 1965 in "Where No Man Has Gone Before," the second *Star Trek* pilot. Haynes had just a supporting role in that as the Communications Officer. Nimoy also worked in *Assault On The Wayne* with another of his old *Star Trek* co-stars as William Windom had guest-starred in "The Doomsday Machine." Then there's Malachi Throne who played Commodore Mendez in "The Menagerie. "

THE MAN BETWEEN THE EARS

Leonard Nimoy in MISSION IMPOSSIBLE

In *Assault On The Wayne* Leonard gets to do a lot of shouting and chewing people out in his role as a by-the-book commander who can be counted on to get the job done. He does a good job but the role lacks dimension. A small character bit about his ex-wife comes up once early in the story and then is neatly tied up at the end without exploration. A flashback sequence involving his wife (perhaps as a fever-dream) would have added to his character. The film isn't terrible; Nimoy picks his post-*Star Trek* roles carefully. In fact Leonard's TV appearances during the Seventies are few and far between. Leonard was constantly trying to reshape his

career without resorting to endless guest-starring roles.

His participation in *Catlow* was pleasant. When he was called by the film's producer, he was distracted developing a photographic print; success had enabled him to revive his youthful interest in photography. He realized that, after nearly ten years, he had been offered work in a feature film. (He had been in the 1967 film *Valley of Mystery*, but that was actually an unsold television pilot padded out and released theatrically.) *Catlow* was like a vacation; his family accompanied him to Spain, where shooting was to take place, and he carted along his cameras and darkroom supplies, as Spain promised a great deal of photo opportunities. Leonard's old friend and teacher Jeff Corey was also in the cast, which added to the convivial atmosphere.

Catlow broke no new ground; the Western genre was fading into cliché, but for an average Western it was well made, and enjoyable. Leonard has a brief rear-view nude scene as he gets out of a bathtub in full view of the camera. The scene was incidental and not sexual, and soon faded into cinematic oblivion. More important to Leonard's immediate career was the real beard (after all those countless fakes on *Mission: Impossible*) that he'd grown prior to shooting. The director, Sam Wanamaker, had no objection as this was a period piece. The beard was to accompany Leonard to his next role, which would also mark his first substantial stage work since the years before his television success.

8
Actor at Large

Leonard returned to the legitimate stage in a role that took him back to his cultural roots. He took the part of Tevye, the Jewish milkman hero of the popular musical, *"Fiddler On The Roof,"* at the Cape Cod Melody Tent theatre in Hyannis, Massachusetts, beginning in July, 1971. The production played other venues in Massachusetts, in Toledo, Ohio and in East Rochester, New York before completing its run, once again, in Hyannis in September. Leonard almost lost the role due to his other commitments, but won over the show's director, Ben Shaktman, by telling him how closely the story paralleled his own family's history in Russia. When Leonard went to Spain to shoot *Catlow*, he carried along the script of "Fiddler" and a tape of the music he needed to learn. Leonard again demonstrated his commitment to a project.

At the conclusion of the run of "Fiddler On The Roof," Leonard returned to the West Coast. He and Ben Shaktman collaborated again almost immediately, in November 1971, when Shaktman directed Leonard in a production of Robert Shaw's play "The Man In The Glass Booth" at the Old Globe Theatre in San Diego. Leonard's dedication to theatre was unwavering. In fact, he paid for his own lodgings and transportation, the costs of which exceeded the wages the Old Globe paid him. He wasn't in it for the money, but the sheer exhilaration of live theatre.

"The Man In The Glass Booth" is a play about a wealthy Jewish businessman who, obsessed with the horror of the Holocaust, and hounded by "survivors guilt" (the horrible self-questioning of why you have survived while everyone else per-

The part of Tevye, the Jewish milkman hero of the popular musical, "Fiddler On The Roof," offered Leonard Nimoy a chance to bring his Jewish heritage and beliefs to life for a viewing audience, a theme that recurs throughout his career

ished), places himself in the remarkable position of being tried for Nazi war crimes. The truth is revealed in a blistering courtroom drama; the man himself serves as a focus for intense emotion and contradictory viewpoints.

The play was a success, but it generated concern in the Jewish community of San Diego; some feared the play was anti-Semitic. Leonard and others involved with the play met with members of the community, and took part in a number of discussions; it soon became apparent that such concerns were held by few people, and even their doubts were soon dispelled.

Controversy aside, Leonard's performance, and the production as a whole, received excellent reviews. One described Leonard as, "A powerhouse on stage. . . [he] sums up with unflagging energy and insights the nature of an extremely complex, driving personality working through a curious deception his own method for salvation. For two hours, Nimoy remains on stage with no letdown. It is a crackling portrayal, a tour de force that continually builds." Another credits Leonard with delivering ". . . a superlative performance. . . as the self-proclaimed Messiah posing as a Jew posing as an ex-Nazi at a war crimes trial in Israel." Most reviews still made reference— frequently in their headlines—to *Star Trek* or Mr. Spock. One newspaper headlined: "Spock Great Sans Ears."

On the outskirts of Leonard's attention, something remarkable was happening; *Star Trek,* in syndication, was becoming popular. This wouldn't have an immediate financial effect, however, as the actors of *Star Trek* only received residuals for the first several broadcasts of each episode. Still, Leonard's work of the previous decade hadn't left him a pauper, and he did no performing until late the following summer.

In August, 1972, Leonard played the role of Fagin in a production of the musical "Oliver!" at the Melody Top Tent theatre in Milwaukee, Wisconsin. Fagin is often portrayed as an unflattering Jewish stereotype, but Lionel Bart's musical comedy adaptation doesn't stoop to this; instead, the character is possessed of considerable complexity and possesses an inner dignity, despite his squalid circumstances. Leonard's performance was commended by critics for its warmth and presence. Leonard also made two appearances on television in 1972, appearing in a *Night Gallery* episode, and in one segment of a dramatic anthology, *Three Faces of Love*.

The *Night Gallery* episode is virtually a one-man show. The few other actors who appear are only on screen for a couple of minutes. Much of the time, Leonard appears tormented, warring with his own disintegrating psyche and the mysterious presence of a huge, threatening cat. Is it his wife's vengeful spirit? Is it a plot by Barbara (his sister-in-law) to get back at Henry because she imagines he killed his wife? Or is it just his own feverish imagination? The ending points towards one of these as Barbara arrives and acts as if she has no idea anything has happened to Henry while he is lying bloody and dead on the bed upstairs while the little cat she had sent over is keeping him company.

This isn't the first time Leonard has been bedeviled by a cat in a story. He was chased by a monstrous feline in "Catspaw" and encountered a shape-shifting alien who looked like a cat named Isis in "Assignment Earth," both in episodes of *Star Trek*.

There is yet another *Star Trek* connection. The director of the *Night Gallery* episode is Gerry Finnerman, the former director of photography on *Star Trek* who was responsible for the colorful lighting on that series.

9 A Slight Return

In 1973, the *Star Trek* revival bore fruit, if only briefly. Filmation Studios launched a *Star Trek* animated series, ultimately airing in 22 episodes. Gene Roddenberry got his original cast to provide voices, with the sole exception of Walter Koenig; Filmation had to draw the budgetary line somewhere. Two alien beings (who would have been beyond the scope of the live action series) took the place of Chekhov. In an interview given at the time to the *L. A. Free Press* (7/13/73), Leonard seemed uncertain about the project, despite his involvement. The interviewer questioned if the show was going to be exclusively aimed at the children's market. Leonard responded, "We don't know. Unfortunately, I don't have control over the material. I will have control only to the extent that I can refuse to do a script that is sent me and then I am in breach of contract and we start with that whole business again.

"I was in Florida when the whole thing came up and I was contacted by mail and by phone. It was very difficult. All the people who were doing it were here in California, and I was assured by all, my agent and Gene Roddenberry and Dorothy Fontana, who's going to produce the show, that the intention was to do a very special kind of animation to really use the medium properly and successfully and to maintain the quality that *Star Trek* originally was intended to have. And, that the material would be new, fresh, good stuff. We were really going to do it right."

He continued, "Okay. Everybody starts out with good intentions. I have never met a producer or a writer who came to me and said, 'We are going to do something that is going to be so

Leonard
Nimoy
and Susan
Hampshire
in BAFFLED

lousy. . .' Nobody ever says that. I believe that these people mean
it. But when the exigencies set in, they start to turn out some
scripts. They take them to people who are financing it and they
say, 'Oh, wait a minute, we can't do this, I mean, this script would
be terrific for a philosophy department at UCLA, but not for Sat-
urday morning cartoon television. It won't work.' Then the arguments start. And it's a question of how tough they're going to be
and how strong they're going to be in taking a stand on what is
good *Star Trek*."

The animated series proved adequate, nothing more. The
actors usually sounded as if they were reading lines, and the
scripts were bland. An exception was the D. C. Fontana-penned
"Yesteryear," which shows Spock as a boy, while the adult Spock
goes back in time to prevent his younger self from dying and altering history. The young Spock is saved, but his beloved pet is
killed saving the boy. As Leonard had feared, the network wanted
the script altered so that the creature would survive to avoid up-
setting young viewers. This, of course, would have completely undermined the dramatic focus of the story. Fortunately, Fontana
fought for her story; the rest of the scripts didn't fare so well.

This was little more than a diversion for Leonard. Throughout 1973, he continued to perform in regional theatre productions. 1973 also saw the broadcast of the TV movie *Baffled*, which was actually an unsold pilot filmed back in 1971, and of *The Alpha Caper*, a bland, pointless heist picture with Henry Fonda. Leonard also made his directorial debut with a *Night Gallery* episode, "Death on a Barge" (3/4/73).

In February and March of 1973, Leonard travelled to Florida to play opposite Sandy Dennis in a production of Robert Randall's play "Six Rms Riv Vu." This Neil Simon-esque comedy/drama featured him as a married man who has an affair with a married woman he meets while they are both looking at an apartment. (This sounds vaguely like *Last Tango In Paris,* but is played for warmth and humor, not hyper-dramatic angst.)

In July, Leonard returned to Massachusetts, to portray King Arthur in the popular musical "Camelot." Director Otto Preminger saw Leonard's performance and sought his talents for a play he was preparing in Washington, D. C. After a brief engagement playing Fagin again in "Oliver!," Leonard proceeded to the nation's capital to act in "Full Circle."

"Full Circle" was the only play written by German author Erich Maria Remarque, who was best known for his novel *All Quiet On The Western Front* and the films adapted from that book. After the Nazis revoked his German citizenship in 1938, he left Europe and came to the United States. He later married actress Paulette Goddard. All of his work after he came to the United States (where he was naturalized in 1947) was concerned with World War Two and the Nazis. "Full Circle" is no exception.

The play takes place in Berlin, the night of Hitler's death but before the news of his suicide was known. The Red Army is advancing on the city. The setting is the apartment of a woman named Anna (Bibi Andersson), whose husband was killed for helping Jews escape from the Nazi secret police, the Gestapo. In the course of the play, different people show up at Anna's apartment and relate how the war has affected them. One of them,

Rohde (Nimoy), is an escapee from a concentration camp who asks Anna to hide him. The Nazi police show up looking for him soon afterward. They try to get another Jew, named Katz, to identify Rohde, and offer him enticements, but Katz throws himself out a window to his death rather than betray his friend. The drama continues in this vein until Russian troops arrive. One Nazi produces forged papers to pass himself off as a Jew, and tries to convince the Russians that Rohde is a Nazi. The Soviet soldiers are not convinced. In the end, Rohde leaves with them, even though he knows (as any student of history might already know) that his life is at risk with the Russians as well. Leonard, Andersson and the performance in general received excellent reviews in Washington D. C. and in New York City.

1974 saw Leonard continuing his stage appearances, largely in plays he was familiar with: "Oliver," "Fiddler On The Roof," and "Six Rms Riv Vu." His most notable stage portrayal was undoubtedly in May, when he went to Sullivan, Illinois to play R. Patrick McMurphy in the stage adaptation of Ken Kesey's *One Flew Over The Cuckoo's Nest.*

In August, Leonard returned to Milwaukee to play the King of Siam in the musical "The King And I." The only hitch was the presence of hundreds of bats in the upper regions of the theater—but the show was a sell-out and the bats didn't prove a major problem.

In THE ALPHA CAPER, Leonard Nimoy is one of a gang of crooks who plan a brilliant heist

10 | To Spock or Not to Spock

By the middle of the 1970s, interest in a *Star Trek* revival had been steadily growing. Speculation was rife as to whether the principal actors would return to their roles. Although tantalizing statements had come from Gene Roddenberry, nothing had yet materialized, either on television or at the movies. This did not prevent *Star Trek* fanatics from hoping. . . and then, for those who were prone to judge a book by its cover, a bombshell dropped.

In November of 1975, Leonard released an auto-biographical volume entitled *I Am Not Spock*. This was not an assault on the character, instead, Leonard discussed the interaction between the character and the actor, and was quick to credit *Star Trek* with making his success possible. The cover even featured a black-and-white portrait of Leonard, in Spock bangs, giving the Vulcan hand greeting. On the other hand, his ears were completely obscured. Apparently, he wasn't about to go that far, and also did not include any Spock photos amongst the accompanying illustrations of his many roles. Some *Star Trek* fans took this book as an assault on their favorite show, assuming that it meant Leonard would never return to *Star Trek* in any way, shape or form.

One fan wrote a spiteful letter (quoted in *The Soho Weekly*, 8/4/77) that left Leonard feeling attacked. It read, in part:

*"Good for you. Do not return to Star Trek. I approve your pretensions to stardom. I look forward to your wrecking the greatest show of all time with your a****** tactics. Big man, big money, big book. I Am Not Spock. Really fantastic. We all will cheer when you and your fellow star William Shatner gut the En-*

terprise of her captain and executive officer. . . why the hell should the f***** series go on now if you're going to kick it in the groin before production even starts? You and your 'career' can take two running steps straight into hell. We made you and we will unmake you. So you're not Spock, huh? The one, the only slimy character of the 'sixties to be put in the Hall of Fame of Video along with Matt Dillon and Lucy Ricardo when everything else about television is lost to memory fifty years ago [sic], the one bloody character that became an icon to a generation. I got news for you, as long as you live, you will only be known as Spock, Vulcan hero, to a planet of youth. I hereby put a curse on your miserable future career. May 100 million hands turn dials when you appear on the TV screen."

This venom was generated by seeing the title of Leonard's book, as the writer of this letter would have known, if he had actually read the book, that Leonard had never said he would never play Spock again. Leonard was aghast at such barely concealed hatred. In his book he had humorously examined the relationship between himself and the character who made him famous, even going so far as to create imaginary dialogues with his Vulcan alter ego. Although Leonard would, in the end, be the last to sign on when *Star Trek* was finally revived, his reticence was the result of valid business concerns, not of greed, apathy or the hatred of fans that some, like this irrationally angry letter writer, seemed to fear. There is, however, as so many have learned (some in far more tragic ways), the sad and dismal truth that many people somehow think that they own the people who have provided them with entertainment.

A quarter of a century after dropping out of Boston College, Leonard enrolled at Antioch College and began to pursue a degree in education. He also signed a contract to record dramatic readings for Caedmon Records. He made five narrative albums for Caedmon including readings from H. G. Wells' *War of the Worlds* and Ray Bradbury's *The Martian Chronicles*. Apart from a few fanatics, and an atrociously bad TV movie entitled *The Missing Are Deadly*, 1975 seemed a very good year for Leonard; his book sold very well.

Another Brand of Logic

In 1976, Leonard played a character he considers just as alien as Spock: Sherlock Holmes. He had the title role in William Gillette's turn-of-the-century treatment of the sagacious sleuth. "I've always felt I should do Holmes some day," Leonard said at the time. "I think my chemistry, my looks, my image all are helpful in playing that role. Besides, I understand Holmes.

"In his own way, Holmes was very much an iconoclast. He's an asocial man, hardly your average nine-to-five worker with a family. Instead, he's chosen a very special kind of life, and he has very little respect for most of the people around him who are also involved in his profession. He's an outsider in so many ways—particularly in his relationships, or rather lack of relationships, with women. Holmes is very much an alien, all right, and I felt that I could understand him the same way I understood Spock.

"I guess the reason I relate so strongly to characters like that," the actor continued, "has to do with my feelings about myself—the way I perceive things. I've really always considered myself an outsider, ever since I can remember. It wasn't by choice—it just happened. I don't follow trends the way a lot of people do. I'm not gregarious. I don't strike up conversations with people easily. I love my family, of course, and I have some dear friends, but I don't enjoy being around a lot of people, and I've never enjoyed social chatter."

Leonard stepped into Sherlock's shoes with a general understanding of the Holmes character but little familiarity with the detective's actual exploits. He had read neither "The Final Problem" nor "A Scandal In Bohemia," two of the Arthur Conan Doyle sagas which figure in the play.

Leonard Nimoy as that other master of logic, Sherlock Holmes

"In fact," Leonard admitted, "I hadn't read any of the stories. I never was a real Holmes buff. I remember seeing a couple of the movies featuring Basil Rathbone as Holmes, and I'd seen the play when it was on Broadway. But that was about it. I pretty much had to start from scratch. I must say, though, that I've gotten a lot of mail from real Sherlock Holmes fanatics who've seen me in the role and almost all of them have been extremely supportive. Some of the people have written to give me advice on the kind of pipe I should be smoking, or to tell me what sort of cape I should wear. But most of the letters come from people who say I'm a good Holmes.

"Mainly, the way I prepared for the part was simply to read as many of the stories as I could in a big hurry, then try to find my way into the Holmes mystique. The mystique's pretty easy to understand. Holmes is a fascinating character. He has these powers of observation we all would like to think we could develop, if we only knew how.

"And of course," Leonard added, "the world Holmes lives and works in is a very rich and complete one. When you read the stories, you can feel the texture of the place—Baker Street, the

London fog, the boats on the river, the hansom cabs in the streets. It's a wonderful world to step into. The values are very clearcut. The bad guys are totally bad, and the good guys like Holmes and Watson are always thoroughly dependable and incorruptible. It's comfortable, stepping back in time to an era like that. We live in a very different society, obviously. Things aren't so simple. Even when a criminal is caught, justice is a very complicated affair, with all sorts of sociological and psychological aspects entering it."

Leonard saw certain parallels between *Star Trek* and the world of yesteryear occupied by the sleuth of Baker Street. He said, "I think that people are still interested in *Star Trek* for the same reasons they're still interested in Holmes. It presented a complete, credible world just like Doyle's stories do. It didn't play down the viewer's intellect the way some of the space shows like *Lost In Space* did. It wasn't played for fantasy. You had the bad guys and you had problems, but you also had dependable, incorruptible heroes to solve them. Real heroes. And boy, our society sure could use some of them today."

The version of Holmes seen in the play was not the grim character seen in the original Doyle stories. Leonard explained, "What we're doing is a kind of reverent sendup of the whole Holmes thing. I don't think this material could play today otherwise. For instance, there's a scene in which Holmes discovers a con man has tied up a damsel and stuffed her in a closet. When I open the closet and see her, I turn to the con man and say, 'You contemptible scoundrel!' Now in the 1890s, when the play was written, that would have been a very acceptable thing to say and it would have been a dramatic moment. But today it's camp. Everyone laughs. It's a fun kind of play."

At this point in his career, Leonard was concentrating on stage work— the legitimate theatre— and hoped some day to play great roles such as Cyrano de Bergerac. "There are a couple of Shakespearean characters I think I should tackle, too," he observed. "Henry V, for instance, because of the beauty of his speeches and the romance. The style of that character is sensational. But I'm not really obsessed with playing any particular role the way some actors are."

It seemed a natural development that the cool efficient Mr. Spock would become the cool and efficient Sherlock Holmes, thanks to the perspicacity of Leonard. Both Holmes and Spock commanded many of the same character traits, such as a relentless devotion to logic, a strictly dispassionate involvement with the job at hand, and neither character could afford to allow himself to be swayed by any external factors which may arise. A probing and decisive mind backed by a deft intellect marked each character and challenged Leonard to convey this to the viewers. Spock, like Holmes, often depended on intellect and information alone, leaving the guesswork to those less qualified.

Leonard, with his commanding presence and saturnine features, is truly the type of individual who stands out when he enters a room, or walks on stage. He took the character of Spock and built him into a legend. He gave a true dignity to someone totally alien, particularly considering the time period, and fought an uphill battle to make it work. He accomplished much the same thing with Sherlock Holmes. Leonard certainly seemed to have been a logical choice to present the world with the best of two very different and exciting worlds.

While Leonard appeared as Holmes in the play in Los Angeles, California, in Denver, Colorado and in Chicago, Illinois in 1976, the same play travelled to other cities with different performers. John Colicos played Holmes when the play was staged in Miami, Florida and other cities. And when it was taped for airing on Home Box Office it was Frank Langella who essayed the role of Holmes. Each actor brought their own personal mark to the performance, but Leonard's seems to have been the most popular. What he failed to mention in any of his interviews is that the play has an ending uncharacteristic to any Doyle story in that Holmes gets the girl in the end! Whether that makes it an "irreverent sendup" depends on how you define irreverent.

12 Wild Flights & Horse Sense

In 1976, Leonard Nimoy signed on as host and narrator of a new syndicated series entitled *In Search Of. . . .* Perhaps it was his fame as an unassailably logical sort of fellow that led to his participation in this venture, although he claimed a life-long interest in the outré subject matter of the show. Public relations? Maybe. But there's no denying that Leonard's presence lent an air of respectability to a show which featured such diverse topics as UFOs, the Bermuda Triangle, the Loch Ness monster, Easter Island, Atlantis, ghosts, ESP and other dubious fields of study. It was all presented rather straightforwardly; each episode invariably ended with Leonard solemnly questioning whether or not we can really know the relative truth of the issue. More down to Earth mysteries were also examined, from the search for the real-life basis of Sir Arthur Conan Doyle's Sherlock Holmes to the unknown fate of the mysteriously vanished Roanoke Colony of Colonial Virginia. *In Search Of. . .* ran for six years, a runaway success.

In 1977, Leonard agreed to take the demanding role of psychiatrist Dr. Martin Dysart in Peter Shaffer's play "Equus," a deep, absorbing work about a disturbed young man who has blinded six horses. In trying to break through to the troubled youth, Dysart ultimately faces the realization that modern man— and more specifically, Dysart himself— has lost something intangible by ridding himself of his inner demons, and is left feeling empty, no longer certain about the alleged superiority of sanity to madness.

Leonard Nimoy actually filmed more episodes of IN SEARCH OF. . .
than he did for any other television series, including STAR TREK
and MISSION: IMPOSSIBLE. The series offered explorations
into the mysterious world of the near possible.

Leonard Nimoy and Leila Gordon face terror in the remake of INVASION OF THE BODY SNATCHERS

Leonard came to this role after it had been occupied by four great actors: Alec McCowan (who created the role in Great Britain), Anthony Hopkins (now best known as another sort of psychiatrist, the murderously brilliant Dr. Hannibal Lecter of *Silence of the Lambs*), Anthony Perkins (still best known, perhaps, as a *Psycho* of his own), and Richard Burton (whose intense stage presence, unfortunately, did not come across at all in Sidney Lumet's later film adaptation of *Equus)*. Leonard had his work cut out for him.

He decided to focus on the role of horses in the story. Dysart's patient is obsessed with horses; in the play they are represented through mime; the actors playing the horses wear immense, stylized sculptured representations of horses' heads, an intense symbolism harkening back to ancient Greek theatre's ritual use of masks. Indeed, Leonard saw the play as a conflict between modern rational man and primal forces, here represented by a sort of horse god. His approach was to put an ad in *The New York Times*, which asked for a horse psychiatrist to aid him in his research for the role. Out of two hundred applicants from a variety of horse-related fields (jockeys, veterinarians, psychologists, horse trainers and even racing fans) he settled upon a young ethologist named Hedy Strauss to instruct him in the nuances of the equine mind.

He then turned his attentions to his co-star, actor Ralph Seymour. Their characters' conflicts are intense; Leonard adopted an antagonistic stance toward the young actor, in order to fuel their performances. The focus of his wrath was Seymour's heavy smoking, which Leonard rightly pointed as a serious threat to any actor's greatest asset: his voice. He browbeat Seymour into giving up cigarettes— but kept an eye on him and renewed the attack when an attack of bronchitis revealed that Seymour had slipped off the non-smoker's wagon. His own approach to rehearsal was intense; in addition to seven hours at the Helen Hayes Theatre every day, he put in several more intensive hours, occupying his mind with the play 24 hours a day. The work was well worth it, as Leonard's Broadway debut not only generated good reviews but boosted ticket sales by 20%. (This certainly wasn't hindered by one ardent Nimoy fan who attended sixteen performances over a three week period!) Leonard performed the role of Dysart from June to October of 1977.

Although the 1978 remake of *Invasion of the Body Snatchers* garnered mixed reviews and mediocre boxoffice returns, Leonard was singled out as performing some of his best work in years.

13 No Ear Jokes, Please

In 1978, Leonard again showed his versatility in the play "Vincent: The Story of a Hero." "Vincent" is the story of Theo and Vincent Van Gogh's gift of over 1,800 paintings and drawings; a legacy that enriched the world's treasury of art masterpieces. During his lifetime, Vincent was presumed by many to be mad; Theo was a clerkish man with little money. From the perspective of history, they seem to have complimented each other to a great degree, each providing the other with a personality aspect they lacked individually.

Why a play about Vincent Van Gogh? Why was Leonard so obsessed with Vincent's life? He was. He said so. Why did he tell Vincent's story to anyone who would listen, on stage or not? Why Vincent and Theo Van Gogh and not someone else?

Leonard believed them both to be heroes; they did the impossible against all odds. They had no chance but did it anyway. Theo Van Gogh believed that one day his brother Vincent would be to art what Beethoven was to music. How did this clerkish little man know this? Why was Vincent driven to produce the work—1800 pieces over a span of only 12 years? How was Theo always able to provide the financial support that Vincent needed, and the moral support so necessary? They had something to say, and whether or not anyone listened, they did it anyway. Both Vincent and Theo Van Gogh died before the fruition of their dream. "Vincent was different," Theo says, "But you are blessed by that difference, for he gave you beauty. He was not perfect, he was far from perfect, but he strived to accomplish noble things for mankind, and he did."

Vincent Van Gogh's favorite quotation was from Ernest Renan, a French historian and theologian of the time:

To act well in this world, one must sacrifice all personal desires. The people who become the missionaries of religious thought have no fatherland than this thought: Man is not on Earth merely to be happy, nor can he be simply honest. He is here to realize great things for humanity to attain nobility, and to surmount the vulgarity of nearly every individual.

This credo, to accomplish noble things for mankind, attracted Leonard because of his own strong social conscience.

"Vincent: The Story of a Hero" was adapted by Leonard from the play "Van Gogh" by Phillip Stephens. The play was sent to Leonard to read and he said, "I laughed and I cried. I knew I wanted to do it." He bought the rights to the play, researched Vincent and Theo Van Gogh for two years and then rewrote and restructured the play incorporating his own ideas. He hoped to replace his popular college lecture series with "Vincent," working out of a suitcase. He planned to use whatever antique furniture and props were available where he was performing. Leonard took it on a trial run of four cities in 1978, premiering in Sacramento, California on May 18. The other cities on the tour that year were Minneapolis, Milwaukee and Portland. The play was popular and received good reviews. Leonard was able to continue performances through 1981.

The props were only a desk and chair, an easel, a bench, a table, a rug and a straw mat. Also required were a slide projector, a large screen and an audio system. These allowed rear screen projection of slides of Van Gogh's paintings and audio amplification of certain parts of the play. A song by Don McLean, "Vincent" (better known as "Starry, Starry Night,") opens the second act, and also requires the audio system. It was later deleted as a good number of critics had centered comments around the song rather than the play. In fact, at a San Diego performance of "Vincent," there was actually laughter when the song began playing, as though many found it incongruous. They didn't know the song had always been intended to be about Vincent Van Gogh, as did anyone who listened to the lyrics, but when a device attracts more attention than the play, it must go. Leonard substituted the "L'Arlesienne Suite" by Bizet for the introduction to the second act. Van Gogh had spent time in Arles and the music was written about that city. Leonard knew of the piece and wanted to see if it might be suitable; when he went to purchase the record, there was a Van Gogh print on the cover, which left no doubt in his mind.

"Vincent" was rich with information about the two Van Gogh brothers. Vincent wanted to do something noble for mankind and Theo provided support, financial and spiritual, for his brother, while everyone else believed Vincent insane. As Theo, Leonard gave a view of the painter that could never be seen if he were to portray Vincent. "And besides," Leonard frequently quipped, "everyone knows that Kirk Douglas (who portrayed Van Gogh in the 1954 film *Lust For Life*) is Vincent."

Through Theo it was revealed that Vincent was not mad, but epileptic and that many of his problems were related to this. Vincent was, in a manner of speaking, born twice. Van Gogh's mother gave birth to a baby on March 30, 1852, which she named Vincent. The first Vincent died shortly after his birth. Exactly one year later, to the day, another baby was born, and this child was also named Vincent. Young Vincent Van Gogh had to walk past a tombstone which bore his own name every Sunday morning.

Vincent is best revealed in the many letters he wrote to his brother, which Theo kept—over 600 in all. Leonard made good use of parts of these letters; they added dimension to the play. Vincent's many drawings and paintings were shown by rear projection on huge screens. The slides represented an accurate portrayal of the brilliant colors Vincent's paintings are known for.

Although Leonard portrayed Theo, the production belonged to Vincent. It centered on his plight, problems and eccentricities, as well as on his intense love of beauty and nature and his drive to share it with humanity. Leonard's portrayal of Theo never cast a shadow in Vincent's spotlight.

"Vincent" was the perfect vehicle to demonstrate Leonard's many talents. It gave him room to share his marvelous sense of humor, his caring and concern, as well as his great love. This play was a perfect opportunity for him to turn his intensity loose on stage, and to allow it to convey the passion of his interest and concern. One critic said it all: "Vincent is a Nimoy triumph!" Unfortunately, even the kindest reviewers succumbed to the obvious temptation provided by the sight of a man famous for his ears portraying a man famous, in part, for cutting off one of his ears: a Minneapolis critic headlined his text, "We're All Ears For New Nimoy Role."

14 Celestial Reunion

As the '70s neared their end, *Star Trek* ebbed and flowed like a tide. Talk of a movie came and went; Roddenberry's script, "The God Thing," was deemed too controversial by Paramount. A script by Jon Povil was also rejected. Unknown to Roddenberry, Paramount was soliciting scripts from such writers as Robert Silverberg, former *Star Trek* story editor John D. F. Black and Harlan Ellison. Ellison's involvement might have already been compromised, as Roddenberry was not too fond of him, but he withdrew before Roddenberry was even aware of his involvement after the by-now famous incident with a Paramount executive. The exec, who apparently knew nothing about *Star Trek* and less about Ellison, insisted the writer had to add Mayans to his story; Ellison walked out. All these ideas fell through.

In 1976, another *Star Trek* film project, with Philip Kaufman (*The Right Stuff*) directing, was also scuttled. In 1977, Paramount drew up plans for its never-realized "fourth network"—a feat 20th Century Fox would pull off a decade later— and *Star Trek* was to be their prime property. Another *Star Trek* series was put into development. All the principals signed to reprise their roles— except Leonard Nimoy.

Some of the more virulent Spock fans undoubtedly thought, once more, Leonard was trying to scuttle the Enterprise. In truth, his primary reasons had nothing to do with the character or *Star Trek*. He was reticent to get caught up once again in the rigors of filming a weekly television series. His other reason was money; over the years Paramount had made a great deal of money from

Star Trek memorabilia, books and other tie-ins, and residuals from syndication, which Leonard and the other *Star Trek* actors had no part of. The likeness of Nimoy-as-Spock, arguably (along with the Enterprise) the most recognizable image associated with the show, had been used countless times to generate income. Leonard wanted a resolution of this situation, for he felt he deserved compensation for the use of *his* face. This didn't keep Roddenberry from hoping Leonard would make guest appearances on the new *Star Trek* series. (It should be pointed out that Leonard's complaint was with the studio, not Roddenberry.)

The plans went on. Spock's absence was to be explained by his departure to head the Vulcan Science Academy. A new Vulcan character, Lt. Xon, was created; an actor was even hired to play the part. (The character would finally make it to the screen and be killed off in the first few minutes of *Star Trek: The Motion Picture.*)

The studio kicked off the series with a two-hour TV-movie which could be released theatrically in Europe. A script submitted by Alan Dean Foster was given the green light. Then Paramount chief Michael Eisner dropped a bombshell on Roddenberry: the movie *had* to have Spock. Roddenberry, convinced *he* and no one else was *Star Trek*, did not care for the idea. He believed his creation could fly without Leonard Nimoy— and without William Shatner, too, if it came to that. Eisner was adamant. If only from the promotional point of view, Spock was irreplaceable. Eisner was even willing to offer Leonard one hundred thousand dollars for three days work, just to include Spock in a small number of scenes. Negotiations were underway to get Leonard in the movie and a limited number of episodes, and to settle his case against Paramount.

The project was rolling; sets were built; scripts poured in. Then Paramount couldn't sell commercial time because the other three networks cut their rates. The fourth network was scuttled, along with plans to revive *Star Trek*. Plans for a feature film were bandied about but abandoned early in 1977.

Suddenly Paramount changed direction again. Steven Spielberg's *Close Encounters of the Third Kind* was a huge success, and they realized, after regarding George Lucas' *Star Wars* as a fluke, that a major science fiction feature could make them money. A feature film, of course, would need state of the art special effects, so they geared up for motion picture production.

Public interest in *Star Trek* was high and some fans regarded Leonard as a spoiler. In September of 1978, Leonard's office was broken into three times. After the third burglary, the police nabbed a suspect. Teresa Victor, still working for Leonard, identified the stolen property. The judge drew her aside and asked her what was happening with *Star Trek*.

Finally Leonard settled his grievances with Paramount Pictures when he signed for *Star Trek: The Motion Picture* and reportedly received $3. 5 million, which included the settlement of his dispute with the studio. *Star Trek* was back on line after nearly a decade of absence. Robert Wise (*The Day The Earth Stood Still*) directed from a Gene Roddenberry script which incorporated elements of the Alan Dean Foster script and other treatments.

In retrospect, *Star Trek: The Motion Picture* hardly seemed worth the wait. The cast did a good job; the failure lay in an almost absurdly pious approach to *Star Trek*, and shameless wallowing in expensive special effects.

In June of 1979, Leonard sponsored a family reunion in Boston. His father's sister finally arrived from Odessa, after a 58 year separation from her family. In 1980, he made a single TV-movie appearance in *Seizure: The Story of Kathy Morris*.

In April of 1981, Leonard was invited by NASA to witness the shuttle *Columbia* landing at Edwards Air Force Base. He had previously appeared at Cape Canaveral along with Gene Roddenberry and other *Star Trek* cast members in honor of the naming of the first space shuttle *The Enterprise*. Due to misinformation passed to the people behind the "Name-the-shuttle-the-Enterprise" campaign, the first space shuttle was never actually

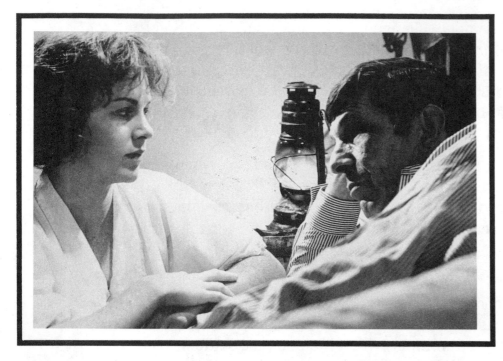

Again reflecting his heritage, Leonard Nimoy played the husband of Golda Meir, a former prime minister and a founding "father" of Israel. The young Meir was portrayed by Judy Davis

launched into space, and instead was only launched from a 747 to test the landing capabilities of the spacecraft.

Late in 1981, production began on *Star Trek II: The Wrath of Khan*. This film was to provide a good deal more action than the first one, as Kirk's old TV nemesis Khan (Ricardo Montalban) returned to wreak general havoc. (The film contains a notable error. Khan is discovered by Chekov, and Khan recognizes him. . . even though Walter Koenig did not join the cast of *Star Trek* until a season after Khan's first appearance.) This time, the director would be Nicholas Meyer (*Time After Time*). As production proceeded, however, a rumor grew which provoked upheavals in the hearts of fans everywhere. Supposedly, Spock was going to die.

The rumor was, of course, absolutely true. Many diehard fans felt this should *not* happen. Had they really waited all this time for *Star Trek* to come back only to lose Spock the second time out? Leonard began to receive threatening and unpleasant letters. The reason for the planned death was, initially, that making the first *Star Trek* movie had been an unpleasant experience for Leonard, and he wanted to break away from the series. Although it was his idea, he has maintained that it wasn't. Ironically Leonard had such a pleasant time making the *Wrath of Khan* he would prove quite amenable to returning after all. The fan pressure, however, was so intense Paramount began doubt their script during the last two weeks of shooting. Director Meyer swore he would walk off the film if they dropped their commitment to the shooting script, and the death remained. Cast and crew present at the shooting of the death scene were actually reduced to tears, a phenomenon repeated at the screenings of the dailies. Early drafts of the script had Spock dying halfway through the picture, but Walter Koenig accurately pointed out this would work better dramatically if Spock's death formed the climax of the film. Anything that followed the death would be anticlimactic.

In the final days of shooting, a group of *Star Trek* fans put together enough money to take an ad in a major Hollywood trade paper to implore Paramount not to kill Spock. Such a move, they said, would cause the film to take a nosedive at the boxoffice and lose millions of dollars.

They were dead wrong. The second *Star Trek* film was both a financial and critical success. Many consider it to be the best of the series.

1982 also saw Leonard in important roles in two television mini-series, *A Woman Called Golda* and *Marco Polo*. These had been made under his package deal with Paramount wherein he signed to do the second *Star Trek* film only as part of a three picture deal to include appearances on non-Trek related projects as well.

In June of 1982, Leonard received the Award of Excellence from the Film Advisory Board. Later that year, NASA honored him with a plaque presented at the Jet Propulsion Laboratories.

15

Behind The Camera

When approached about doing *Star Trek III,* Leonard mused that he would like to direct. After all, he knew more about *Star Trek* and its characters than either of the two preceding directors. To his surprise, Paramount chief Michael Eisner thought it a great idea. Leonard *had* directed before, after all, for a *Night Gallery* episode in 1973, an episode of Harve Bennett's short lived *Powers Of Matthew Star* series in 1982, and a *T. J Hooker* episode in 1983.

Oddly enough, no one questioned Leonard's ability to work with action, special effects or any of the more technical aspects of filmmaking. There was, however, much concern about how he would work with his fellow actors. In a *People Magazine* interview, he said, "I think I know when they've been well used and when they've been ill used. I could call on them to do things that others might not know were there."

Still, he encountered competitiveness from the rest of the cast, prompted by his apparent rise to a place of power. This soon dissipated as it became readily apparent he wasn't on an ego trip but serious about doing the best job possible. James Doohan would later comment, "He comes [to the set] with his homework done, the cinematographer's homework done, and if you allow him to, he would show you that he has your homework done, too. He's really terrific."

Fears that Shatner would be out of sorts proved unfounded. He wanted to increase his input into the script, but was perfectly

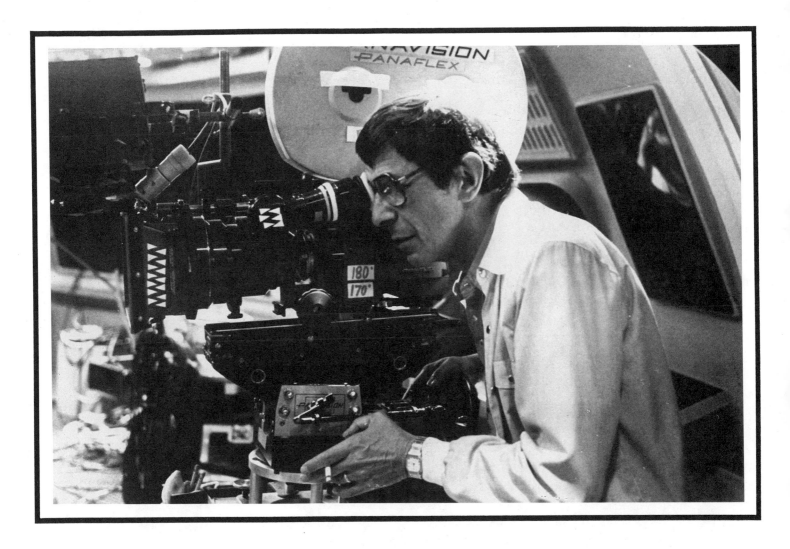

Leonard Nimoy behind the cameras directing THE SEARCH FOR SPOCK

affable when he discovered Leonard was open to discussion. The two had enjoyed years of friendship. An amusing incident in shooting demonstrated their cooperation. William Shatner had a big scene coming up, so Leonard asked everyone else to leave the set while he and Shatner discussed it. They then proceeded to stage a mock fight for the benefit of the rest of the cast and crew, cursing each other loudly and throwing things around. In reality, it was all a put-on.

Fortunately for Leonard the director, Leonard the actor only appeared at the end of the film. It was readily apparent that directing one's self can be excruciatingly difficult. Leonard relied on Harve Bennett, William Shatner and others to help him.

"The biggest problem I had," he observed later, "and this is really silly, but it happens that it was the scene in the sick bay of the bird of prey. Spock is unconscious and McCoy is talking to him. Now, not only am I in the scene, but I have to play the scene with my eyes closed. So I can't even look to see if the actor I am playing the scene with is looking anything like I think he should look. It drove De Kelley crazy. He swears that I was trying to direct him with the movement and flutter of my eyelids. It was very difficult. In a sense I was very pleased and relieved that the design of the story allowed me to do a minimal amount of performing."

Leonard assessed himself as a director by saying, "I'm probably somewhere in between Bob Wise and Nicholas Meyer. Not as precise as Bob, not as imaginative or rough edged as Nick. I think the major difference, and for me the most important difference, is my attitude toward the story and the actors. They [Wise and Meyer] are looking for a different kind of final product than I am."

The studio had problems with the movie. Roddenberry's idea to have the youthful, reborn Spock go through his first *pon farr* again seemed crucial, but the studio didn't understand it. Fortunately, Leonard and Harve Bennett stuck it out, and the scene remained. Some complaints were even more trivial. The studio complained about all the smoke on the bridge of the Klingon ship.

Harve Bennett was obliged to show Paramount a clip from their own smash hit *Flashdance*, in which the main character dances in an artistic-looking smoke filled room— even though there was only one person smoking in the scene. Paramount, embarrassed, backed down.

The fans, too, wanted a hand in the filmmaking process. Once again, a true rumor leaked out: that the Enterprise was going to be destroyed. As before, an outcry was raised. . . to no avail.

Star Trek III: The Search For Spock was a hit, amassing as much money as its predecessor. Leonard's bag of tricks was doubled; he had proven himself as both actor (over a thirty year period) and director.

1984 also saw Leonard make an appearance in a supporting role in a television mini-series remake of *The Sun Also Rises,* which aired in December. He guest starred in the role of The Count, a character who didn't appear in the original version of the film. In adapting the novel for television, the producers opted to avoid the straightforward adaptation done in the Tyrone Powers version of the Fifties and instead added a dramatic subplot which involved introducing a completely new character to the story, played by Leonard. Regarding his place in the story, he told Jim Brown on NBC (12/7/84), "Redoing a piece of material is valid if there's a good reason for doing it, if you feel something fresh and new can be done with it. But. . . if somebody were to say to me how would you like to work with a remake of the *Treasure Of Sierra Madre,* I'd say no thank you, I'll pass on that one. That's been done definitively. " In *People* (9/84), Nimoy went on to explain, "The need for a suspense line was obvious. Without it you have a lovely mood piece, which is what the book was. It needs a climactic moment, which is what the Count provides. "

The TV movie received mixed reviews; *Star Trek III: The Search For Spock* was a hit.

16 Honor And Change

January 16, 1985 was a special day for Leonard. In fact, it was *officially* Leonard Nimoy Day in Los Angeles, by direct declaration of Mayor Tom Bradley. The occasion was the dedication of the 1,796th star on Hollywood Boulevard. Most of the cast of *Star Trek* was in attendance, except for James Doohan, who was ill, and William Shatner, who sent a congratulatory telegram. Shatner was actually just over the hill at the Burbank Studios filming *T. J. Hooker* but felt he couldn't get away even though Leonard had appeared at Shatner's Star ceremony. (A star had already been awarded to William Shatner; Gene Roddenberry and George Takei would receive stars of their own on the Walk of Fame in 1985.) Leonard's thank you speech was basic yet elegant. He simply said, "Thank you very much. Thank you. There are a lot of people to thank. Esther Lemay, and so many people who really got behind this thing and made today happen. So many, many people who really got behind this thing and made today happen. So many, many people who have been so supportive, fans and friends, for such a long time. And, of course, to Mayor Bradley and to Peggy Stevenson and all the people who've honored me here today. I'm very grateful. I'm a very lucky guy. It was about thirty five years ago. . . I was eighteen years old, when the *Enterprise* hadn't been built yet. I came out here from Boston by train. And it was a long ride. It was three days and three nights in a coach seat to arrive in the city of Los Angeles with one hope, and that was to make a living as an actor. A lot of great things have happened. I've been very fortunate to work with so many talented people and to develop such good friends among my co-

workers. I have the love and support of a wonderful family all these years, and I must tell you that there's no way in the world that I ever could have hoped or possibly dreamed that a day like this would come in my life to see this event take place. I'm very grateful for it. As of today, I find myself in a rather illogical condition. I'm probably the only man on this street who can say that his head is in space and his star is on the ground. I want to thank you all very, very much. Live long and prosper."

Leonard's star is located at 6651 Hollywood Boulevard, near the intersection with Cherokee. It is next to the star bearing the name Phil Harris.

In 1986, Leonard returned to his dual roles of Spock and big-time director with *Star Trek IV: The Voyage Home*. This time he was deeply involved in the story from the start, working on a treatment in collaboration with Harve Bennett. Fate threw a strange curveball into the works, however; Eddie Murphy loved *Star Trek* and wanted to be in the next one. Leonard and Bennett

Leonard Nimoy at his Hollywood Star Ceremony

photo by
Della Van Hise

thought about it. So far, they had decided to take the *Enterprise* crew back to the Twentieth Century, and planned to shoot for a lighter sort of story after the death and resurrection of Spock. Maybe Murphy was a good idea. The studio wasn't too sure; Eddie Murphy and *Star Trek* were their biggest money makers, and combining them into one blockbuster might actually reduce their cash returns. Murphy was keen on the idea and story development kept him in mind, as a con man character who gets embroiled with Kirk, Spock and crew.

When Michael Eisner left Paramount for Disney, Leonard found his vistas expanding. Eisner's iron rule about *Star Trek* had been that it *had* to have a definite villain; with the studio chief gone off to greener pastures, there was no such restriction. It left plenty of room for Leonard to develop his plot in less adversarial ways. After all, some of the best *Star Trek* episodes hadn't had a villain. Why should this one?

Meanwhile, *Beverly Hills Cop* screenwriter Dan Petrie, Jr. came in on the project, only to be lured away by the departed Eisner. Another Murphy-centered screenplay was put into the works. Then William Shatner's contract expired on the delayed film and it took the studio six months to negotiate a new salary with him. Harve Bennett came up with the idea of doing a Starfleet Academy flashback to when the *Star Trek* heroes first met, but this was mercifully shelved. The Eddie Murphy script was canned, too, as it soon became apparent the *Star Trek* characters were merely providing support for Murphy. Although the writers of this script still retain screen credit, the script was completely rewritten by Harve Bennett and Nicholas Meyer. (Meyer was overheard at a screening of *Star Trek IV* explaining that Bennett wrote all the serious parts and he wrote all the funny ones, since Bennett, apparently, can't write comedy.)

Leonard himself contributed the notion of the whales. The problem was to figure out what, exactly, the cast was going back in time for. A rare plant required to produce a vitally needed medicine was considered, but somehow a plant didn't seem too dynamic, and when the idea of humpback whales came up, it seemed a natural.

The final product (after the most pleasant *Star Trek* shooting experience to date) gave the whole cast a chance to be involved in the action; Leonard's direction produced some of their finest ensemble work.

In December of 1986, The opening of *Star Trek IV* to an eventual hundred million dollar domestic gross was not the only momentous event in the life of Leonard Nimoy. After thirty-three years of marriage, Leonard separated from his wife Sandi to move in with Susan Bay, a production executive with a young son. Divorce proceedings were begun a few months later.

The year that followed was a difficult one for Leonard. In June of 1987, Leonard accompanied *Star Trek IV* to the U.S.S.R. (a nation once occupying much of Eastern Europe and parts of Asia), to a screening commemorating an international moratorium on whaling. The Soviet government allowed him to visit the family his parents came from— where he found some Nimoys who had stayed behind. He returned to the United States laden with audio recordings and photographs, only to have his father Max die seven days later. His mother Dora faded away after that, dying quietly in December. The tabloids fussed over these events, but Leonard's grief and guilt were private, and only obliquely alluded to in interviews. He continued to work, and his success as a director on two *Star Trek* films led to more offers.

Although he was given the chance to direct both *Lethal Weapon* and *Stakeout*, he wasn't interested in making action-oriented movies, and opted instead to direct *Three Men And A Baby* when the originally slated director, Coline Serreau (who directed the original French film) dropped out, supposedly due to illness. "I thought the original was a very French film with flat characters," said Leonard of the movie, "so I set out to flesh them out and make an American version. . . . I don't find it difficult directing comedy. Some people may be surprised about me doing a comedy, but I have experience theatrically doing it, although I am not known for playing it."

Working with an infant, or rather two, as twins split the role of the infant Mary, was an interesting challenge for Leonard. He explained, "[The baby] didn't know she was being paid to do this. You know, writers have an interesting way of doing these things. They write, 'There the baby laughs; there the baby cries,' but they don't write how to get her to do it. We filmed for two and a half months. She was four and a half months old when we started, so by the time we finished, she had spent one third of her life with us." Getting the baby to cry was actually very difficult at first. . . until the infant realized crying was a great way to get attention

Three Men And A Baby, released in 1987, was a huge success and grossed over $100 million. Work on his fourth directing stint, *The Good Mother* (starring Diane Keaton), held up his participation in *Star Trek V*, delaying the start of that film to late 1988. He even told William Shatner he was free to go ahead and make the film without him but Shatner exploded, "You know I can't make a *Star Trek* movie without you!" While Shatner had not proven inordinately difficult when Leonard was director, he was rather difficult as a director as he felt the pressure of the production every minute and brought more than an average tenseness to the set. Leonard was unhappy from the earliest stages of the story discussion, dismissing the first draft as being so bad it would get them laughed out of the theatre, and later continuing his ongoing complaints over a brother for Spock suddenly being brought in out of left field after twenty some years of *Star Trek* continuity. Making Sybok Spock's half-brother only partially eased his concerns.

In December 1988, when *Star Trek V* was in production, Leonard's second non-*Star Trek* directorial feature film, *The Good Mother* starring Diane Keaton and Liam Neeson, was released to lacklustre reviews and poor boxoffice. In light of the huge success that *Three Men And A Baby* had been, the film was a real disappointment. His next directorial outing, *Funny About Love*, also received mixed reviews and poor boxoffice receipts when it was released in 1990. Although Gene Wilder gave a fine performance and the film is tightly directed, the script was weak and too much of the humor fell flat while the drama seemed contrived rather than natural. If anything, it received even less attention than *The Good Mother* and faded quickly from theaters.

On New Year's Day, 1989, Leonard Nimoy and Susan Bay were married.

In March 1989, Leonard sued *Newsweek* magazine and Pioneer Electronics over their use of a photo of him as Spock in a stereo advertisement.

Star Trek V: The Final Frontier, released in June 1989, did not fare as well as Leonard's two *Star Trek* directorial efforts. Although the cast was in good spirits, the story rambled and often involved the long-running characters in scenes which violated their basic natures. The series was not irrevocably damaged and *Star Trek VI: The Undiscovered Country*, written and directed by Nicholas Meyer, was much better received.

Leonard appeared as Ambassador Spock in a two-part *Next Generation* story in November 1991.

Although the revival of *Star Trek* gave Leonard additional career opportunities, he has demonstrated he has found life after the *Enterprise*. In April 1991, he starred in, and co-produced, the television movie *Never Forget*, a drama about a Holocaust survivor's legal battles against a racist group claiming that the Holocaust never happened. Obviously, Leonard still remains true to his convictions and to his religious roots; after sixty years, he is still going strong. Clearly, even though Spock gave his career impetus, Leonard Nimoy is not entirely dependent on him for his livelihood. If, as is highly possible, his involvement with *Star Trek* ended with *Star Trek VI*, there is still no end in sight for this intelligent actor and director. He will certainly continue to bring his keen mind and dedication to bear on whatever projects he undertakes in the future.

Episodic TV Credits

{This appendix lists Nimoy's known work in episodic television, including some directorial work. Full-length TV pilots that did not lead to a series are discussed in greater length in the Feature Film appendix. Some earlier TV shows are hard to come by, especially the many short-lived syndicated programs produced by ZZIV Productions. Nimoy appeared on many of these as a ZIV contract player, at union scale, which accounts for his many appearances on ZIV's one great success, **Sea Hunt**.

Star Trek, Mission Impossible and **In Search Of. . .** are listed in separate appendices.}

BAFFLED
Unsold pilot, aired NBC, 1/30/73. See Feature Films appendix.

BIG TOWN
Nimoy played a thug in a 1953 episode of this newspaper drama.

BONANZA
The long-running saga of the Cartwright family.

(12/17/60) "The Ape" A take on *Of Mice and Men;* Arnie, a childlike man, is befriended by Hoss, but later accidentally kills a woman he likes. Nimoy plays Freddy, a sleazy character who claims to have tried to save the woman, and who leads the lynch mob that kills Arnie despite Hoss' efforts to save him.

CAIN'S HUNDRED
A crime series based on actual gangland-related cases.

(2-6-62) "Murder by Proxy" Nimoy plays the supporting role of Ralph Tomek in this story of a murder case that runs up against a seemingly foolproof alibi: the accused killer was in jail at the time of the crime.

COLT .45
This series was about Chris Colt (Wade Preston), a government agent travelling in the guise of a gun salesman.

(6/28/59) "Night of Decision" While tracking an outlaw, Colt is captured by the outlaw's mother and brother Luke (Leonard Nimoy).

COLUMBO
Peter Falk's rumpled but infallible detective.

(1/11/73) "A Stitch in Crime" Nimoy plays Dr. Mayfield, a heart surgeon who tries to kill a colleague by using a dissolving suture on his victim in an operation. A nurse discovers this but Mayfield kills her and tries to make it look like she was an addict. Columbo comes in on the case; Mayfield points him towards a friend of the nurse, who is an ex-drug user, and then kills that man with an overdose of morphine, too. He gives the man the fatal shot in the left arm— not realizing that this victim is left-handed, and would inject himself in his *right* arm. Columbo realizes that the overdose was murder, and closes in on Mayfield; Mayfield performs another operation on his rival and replaces the dissolving suture with a good one, but Columbo finds the bad suture, which links the doctor to the other two murders. Another case solved. . .

COMBAT

Vic Morrow starred as Sergeant Saunders, leader of an Allied platoon in WW II Europe.

(10-22-63) "The Wounded Don't Cry" Nimoy plays Private Neumann, who acts as translator. In this episode, Sgt. Saunders risks cooperating with an enemy sergeant in order to get much-needed plasma for both German and American wounded.

(12/28/65) "The Raider" Nimoy plays Private Baum; the platoon must decide how to rescue a captured American officer.

CRIME

Unsold pilot, aired 10/6/73. See *The Alpha Caper* in Feature Film appendix. Writer Stephen Bochco would later star actor James B. Sikking in his successful *Hill Street Blues* series; Executive Producer Harve Bennett would later be vital in the *Star Trek* features, which, needless to say, involved Nimoy as well.

DANIEL BOONE

Fess Parker starred as the famous frontiersman.

(1/13/66) "Seminole Territory" Boone and his Indian friend Mingo (Ed Ames) travel to Florida, where they fall in with a travelling magician. Seminole chief Ottawa and his son Oontah (Nimoy) attack, but the chief is impressed with the magician's tricks. Oontah is not, but obeys his father when he makes the magician an honored guest. Various troubles develop, but Boone works things out with the Chief and all ends well.

DEATH VALLEY DAYS

A Western anthology series.

(6/29/65) "The Journey" A group of Indians is being moved by the Cavalry. One leader, Yellow Bear (Nimoy) wants to break free; another leader opposes him. In the conflict that follows, Yellow Bear is killed by his fellows, who have decided to accept the ascendancy of the encroaching whites.

DRAGNET (NBC)

Sgt. Joe Friday (Jack Webb) and his partner Frank Smith (Ben Alexander) crack tough cases in L.A.

(1/21/54) "The Big Boys" The story involved juvenile delinquents. Presumably, Nimoy was one of them.

DR. KILDARE

Richard Chamberlain starred as the idealistic young doctor.

(5/16/63) "An Island Like A Peacock" Nimoy plays Harry, a sensitive young man in love with a troubled blind girl. His feelings only add to the difficulties which develop when her estranged father, now ill, tries to come back into her life before he dies.

87TH PRECINCT

A series based on Ed McBain's detective novels.

(12/4/61) "The Very Hard Sell" Nimoy plays Barrow, a suspect in the killing of a used-car salesman.

ELEVENTH HOUR

A series starring Ralph Bellamy as part of a psychiatric crisis team.

(12-18-63) "La Belle Indifference" Nimoy plays Detective Cardell, who becomes involved in the case of a disturbed woman who abandoned her child.

(4/22/64) "The Color of Sunset" Buck Denholt (Edmond O'Brien) suffers from tension headaches; perhaps the cause is his fear of being replaced by a younger man, Bart Pelco (Nimoy).

FAVORITE STORY (Syndicated)

A dramatic anthology program.

(6/21/53) "The Adoption" This episode of this anthology series involved a Portuguese family. The wives of the two Castro brothers both give birth to sons on the same night; a local noblewoman offers to raise the sons, but promises to let them choose where to live when they grow up. One mother refuses this offer but the other accepts. The two families quarrel, and a wall divides the Castro lands. Twenty years later, Manuel, who went with the Conteza, returns home. Miguel is angry that his parents kept him from having such a luxurious upbringing. The two cousins meet by the wall and fight, but ultimately reconcile and tear down the wall. Presumably, Nimoy played one of the two cousins, but records do not indicate which one.

FIRESIDE THEATRE (or FIRESIDE ARENA THEATRE)

Not to be confused with the Firesign Theatre. Nimoy appeared on this dramatic anthology series some time in 1950 or '51.

FOUR STAR PLAYHOUSE

A rotating anthology series, both comedy and drama. Nimoy appeared in 1953.

THE GATHERING (PILOT, NOT AIRED)

(12/69) Produced by Allen Ludden, with Nimoy and his son Adam (thirteen years old at the time). Not to be confused with the Ed Asner/ Maureen Stapleton TV-movie aired in December 1977.

GET SMART

Don Adams starred as bumbling spy Maxwell Smart.

(1/22/66) "The Dead Spy Scrawls" Nimoy plays Stryker, a KAOS agent who is always one step ahead of Maxwell Smart—until, as always, Smart triumphs almost in spite of himself.

GUNSMOKE

TV's longest running prime-time series starred James Arness as Marshal Matt Dillon for 20 years.

(12/30/61) "A Man A Day" Cooner and his men plan to steal gold in Dodge City, but need to get Matt Dillon out of the way, so they threaten to shoot a citizen a day until the Marshall gets out of town. Nimoy plays the supporting role of Grice.

(4/23/63) "I Call Him Wonder" Nimoy plays the role of Holt, in a story of an Indian boy out of place in Dodge City.

(4/16/66) "Treasure of Johnny Walking Fox" Nimoy plays the title role. Prejudice makes outcasts of buffalo hunters Jacob Beamus and his Indian friend, Walking Fox.

HARBOR COMMAND (A ZIV Production)

Coast Guard drama starring Wendell Corey. Nimoy appeared in 1954.

HARBORMASTER (aka ADVENTURES AT SCOTT ISLAND)

Another ZIV production, starring Barry Sullivan as a New England coastal cop. Nimoy appeared in 1957.

HIGHWAY PATROL (A ZIV Production)

Broderick Crawford starred as Dan Mathews

(1957, title unknown) Nimoy plays a thug who leans on mill workers dissatisfied with their working conditions.

(1/28/58) "Hot Dust" A young worker (Nimoy) believes that he's been contaminated by radioactive material and goes into hiding; complications ensue.

KRAFT SUSPENSE THEATER

A dramatic anthology.

(10/1/64) ""The World I Want" Nimoy plays Lawrence Brody, a lawyer who helps an old man prepare his will. The old man hates his wife and leaves all his money to his niece Fern, except for five dollars to the wife, since state law requires that he leave her *something*. The wife finds out and kills her husband; she plans to kill Fern as well, but is thwarted by her late husband's deaf-mute handyman.

(4/29/65) "Kill No More" Dr. Clay (Lew Ayres) is obsessed with creating a bomb that will deter wars. Nimoy plays the role of Cowell.

LARAMIE

A Western centered around two orphaned brothers and their ranch. Songwriter Hoagie Carmichael played a leading role in the 1959 season.

(2/20/62) "The Runt" Nimoy plays one of three outlaw brothers who intrude upon the peaceful life of their law-abiding step-brother.

THE LIEUTENANT

Gene Roddenberry's peacetime Marine Corps drama, which starred Gary Lockwood as Lieutenant William Rice.

(2/29/64) "In the Highest Tradition" Rice researches his platoon's history and learns that it was wiped out in a WW II battle. Only one man, Lt. Peter Booney, survived. Nimoy plays Hollywood director and actor Greg Sanders, who wants to make a movie about the wartime incident. The Marine Corps likes the idea but Booney is reluctant to cooperate; Rice discovers that Booney blames himself for the death of his companions, as he was not with the platoon at the time. When Sanders tries to change the story too much, Booney publicly admits his feelings of guilt. Sanders reworks the story so that Booney is shown trying his best to reach his platoon; Booney realizes that he was not a coward, but actually did everything he could under the circumstances.

LOCK-UP

A lawyer series starring Macdonald Carey

(5/13/59) "Morality and the Shield" Nimoy plays Nino Baselice, one of three youths who steal a gun from a cop named Crotty and wind up killing another policeman who interrupts them in a robbery. Crotty faces murder charges, but lawyer Herb Maris (MacDonald Carey, star of the series) looks into the case and eventually clears the innocent man.

LUKE AND THE TENDERFOOT (UNSOLD PILOT)

(8/6/65) A Western comedy, starring Edgar Buchanan as a crooked peddler and featuring Nimoy (as Clyde Meekam) and Michael Landon (as Sherrill).

(8/13/65) A revised, second pilot in which Landon and Nimoy switched roles.

[Cast information from *The Leonard Nimoy Compendium*, which erroneously dates the pilot in 1959. Dates from Goldberg's *Unsold Television Pilots*, which does not list Nimoy in either cast, but lists Charles Bronson in the second pilot, as outlaw John Wesley Hardin.]

A MAN CALLED SHANENDOAH

Robert Horton played a man left for dead after a gunfight; afflicted with amnesia, he takes the name "Shanendoah" and wanders the West for clues to his identity.

(1/10/66) "Run, Killer, Run" Someone's out to kill Shenendoah, but he doesn't know why. Nimoy plays the role of Del Hillman in this story set in Galveston, Texas.

THE MAN CALLED X (A ZIV production)

This espionage show starred Barry Sullivan in the title role. Nimoy appeared in 1954.

THE MAN FROM U.N.C.L.E.

Robert Vaughn and David McCallum as TV's top spies.

(11/24/64) "The Project Strigas Affair" Nimoy plays Vladek, the aide to communist ambassador Kurasov (Werner Klemperer). U.N.C.L.E. enlist the aid of a young American couple (the husband is played by William Shatner) in their plan to discredit Kurasov; Vladek eventually rises to Kurasov's position when the plan succeeds.

MICHAEL SHANE

A detective drama starring Richard Denning

(10/7/60- syndicated) "A Night With Nora" Nimoy is a cowardly photographer who holds some vital clues to clearing Shane of a trumped-up murder charge.

M-SQUAD

This police series starred Lee Marvin.

(4/17/59) "The Firemakers" Nimoy plays a young man who helps police snare his own father, who has committed arson. The young man does this to gain control of the family business. In an interesting piece of casting, Nimoy's father is played by James Coburn.

(5/24/60) "Badge for a Coward" A cop is accused of cowardice when his partner (Nimoy) is shot.

NAVY LOG

(5/22/56) "Sacrifice" In this true maritime drama, an Admiral risks a deadly ocean storm to bring in two hundred planes. Nimoy plays the supporting role of Steven Henderson.

NIGHT GALLERY

Rod Serling's horror anthology series.

(12/24/72) "She'll Be Company for You" Nimoy plays Henry Auden, a man greatly relieved by the death of his sick wife. Barbara, a family friend, senses this and berates him for it, but changes her tune and gives him a small kitten to keep him company. Henry begins to hear a bell from his dead wife's room— the bell she used to summon him. The sound of a tiger roaring also afflicts him. He begins to think he's going mad. He eventually succumbs to the sound of the bell and goes to his wife's room. His body is found, torn and bloodies, with the bloody pawprints of some large cat on the door.

(3/4/73) "Death on a Barge" Leonard Nimoy directed this story, his first job as a director. The story concerns a young man who falls in love with a woman (Leslie Ann Warren) who he only sees at night. A friend believes her to be a vampire, and turns up dead soon afterward. The young man decides to kill her but cannot, as he still loves her; she has spared him because she loves him, too. In the end, her own father drives a stake through her heart, rather than allow the killings to continue.

NOT FOR HIRE

Starred Ralph Meeker as Hawaii-based military cop Sgt. Steve Dekker

(which was also the shows alternative title); Nimoy appeared in 1958.

OUTER LIMITS

Science-fiction/horror anthology.

(4/20/64) "Production and Decay of Strange Particles" An accident at a nuclear plant causes a dimensional rift, and alien entities try to widen the gap; Dr. Marshall (George MacReady) must overcome his own cowardice to reverse the disaster. Nimoy plays the supporting role of Konig.

(11/14/64) "I, Robot" An adaptation of Otto Binder's *Adam Link, Robot* stories. Adam (Read Morgan) is a robot charged with the murder of his creator; Thurman Cutler (Howard Da Silva) is a famous lawyer who defends Link; Judson Ellis (Leonard Nimoy) is a cynical newspaper reporter covering the case. Adam is convicted even though the "murder" is revealed an accident, for the jury cannot deal with his existence. On his way to destruction, the robot breaks free to save a child from a truck, and is himself demolished.

PERRY MASON

TV's infallible detective, played by Raymond Burr.

(1/3/63) "The Case of the Shoplifter's Shoe" Nimoy, like so many others before him, cannot help but break down and confess to murder when faced with Perry Mason's brilliant legal mind.

THE PINKY LEE SHOW

A comedy variety series, in which "stagehand" Lee wound up subbing for performers who didn't show up. Lee was the spiritual ancestor of Pee Wee Herman, and gravitated toward children's TV in the later '50s.

Nimoy appeared on this program some time in 1951.

THE POWERS OF MATTHEW STAR

Harve Bennett created this short-lived fantasy series about an extraterrestrial teenager attending high school on Earth. Just about as good as it sounds.

(2/19/82) "The Triangle" Nimoy directed this episode. Matthew goes to the Bermuda Triangle and discovers mysteries. At least one mystery, Nimoy's involvement in this series, remains unsolved. Note the guest appearance of Nimoy's old friend Jeff Corey.

PROFILES IN COURAGE

Dramatic series based on John F. Kennedy's book.

(12/6/64) "Trial of Richard T. Ely" This is the true story of an American professor (Dan O'Herlihy) who runs into trouble for his views about academic freedom in 1894 Wisconsin. Nimoy plays the young lawyer who defends him, successfully, when a hearing is convened at the university.

RACKET SQUAD
Nimoy appeared on this crime show in 1953.

RAWHIDE
Gil Favor (Eric Fleming) led cattle drives across the West in this popular series; his right-hand man Rowdy Yates (Clint Eastwood) took over for the final season, shortly before going on to international screen stardom.
(5/19/61) "Incident Before Black Pass" Nimoy plays the Kiowa leader Annko, who leads a group of his men off the reservation and takes Rowdy Yates and another cattle driver as hostages.

THE REBEL
This Western series starred Nick Adams as Johnny Yuma.
(11/6/60) "The Hunted" — Nimoy plays Jim Colburn, a friend of Johnny Yuma, who has been jailed for a murder he did not commit. Yuma sets out to clear Jim's name, but Jim panics and escapes. Soon he has a posse on his trail, and Yuma is faced with a difficult situation.

ROUGHRIDERS (A ZIV production)
After the Civil War, three men (2 Union veterans and one Confederate) put their differences behind them and head West together.
(4/30/59) "Gunpoint Persuasion" Lt. Kirby (the Confederate veteran) faces a shotgun wedding, which leads to murder. Nimoy's role is undetermined.

SAM BENEDICT
(10/20/62) "Twenty Aching Years" Nimoy has a supporting role in this courtroom drama.

SEA HUNT (Syndicated— a ZIV production)
ZIV's most (and perhaps only) memorable show, starring Lloyd Bridges as scuba-diving troubleshooter Mike Nelson.
(10/28/58) "The Shipwreck" Nimoy plays Vince Porter, one of several castaways stranded on an island with Mike Nelson.
(11/25/58) "Dead Man's Cover" Mike Nelson concocts a plan to expose Robert Tyler (Leonard Nimoy) as the murderer of his own wife.
(7/14/59) "The Alcatraz Story" Three brothers, including Nimoy as Johnny Brand, dupe Nelson into helping them spring their brother from Alcatraz, but Nelson foils the scheme.
(4/18/60) "Time-Fuse" Nimoy plays Luis Hoyo, who has set fifty tons of dynamite to destroy the harbor of a Latin American country. Mike Nelson must somehow trick Hoyo into revealing the time and place of the explosion.
(5/12/60) "The Invader" Mike Nelson must rescue the president of a Latin American country and thwart a revolution. Nimoy plays the supporting role of Indio Ramirez.

SILENT SERVICE (Syndicated)
Fact-based submarine adventures.
(1954, title unknown) Nimoy plays part of a WW II sub crew who sabotages an enemy railroad.
(7/12/58) "The Tiger Shark" Nimoy plays a sonar operator in this submarine story.

STRANDED (Unsold, unaired pilot, NBC, 1966)
Released theatrically as *Valley of Mystery:* see Feature Film appendix.

TALES OF THE WELLS FARGO

Dale Robertson starred as a troubleshooter for the stagecoach line.

(4/17/61) "Something Pretty" Nimoy plays Jim Coleman, a supporting character.

THE TALL MAN

A series about Pat Garrett and Billy the Kid.

(10/15/60) "A Bounty for Billy" Nimoy plays Deputy John Swift. This was D.C. Fontana's first teleplay.

(1/14/61) "A Gun is for Killing" Nimoy returns as Johnny Swift, only to be killed by a rancher's henchmen.

TATE

Starring David McLean in the title role, a man who wanders the West after losing an arm in the Civil War.

(8/10/60) "Commanche Scalps" A girl named Lucy decides to marry her fiancé's brother (Robert Redford). The jilted bridesgroom decides to kill his brother. Nimoy's role is not known.

THIS MAN DAWSON

An incredibly obscure series, even for ZIV Productions, this show starred Keith Andes as an urban police chief. Nimoy appeared in 1961.

THREE FACES OF LOVE

Unsold anthology pilot, aired 5/1/74, NBC. See Feature Films appendix.

T.J. HOOKER

William Shatner starred as a dedicated street cop who liked to leap on the hoods of speeding cars.

(1/22/83) "The Decoy" Nimoy directed this episode, in which policewoman Stacy (Heather Locklear) acts as a decoy who's been killing young women.

(2/5/83) "Vengeance Is Mine" Nimoy plays a former partner of Hooker's. When Paul McGuire's daughter is raped, he takes the law into his own hands to bring the rapist to justice when he feels that the legal system has failed him.

26 MEN (Syndicated)

(2/13/59) "The Long Trail Home" A Western based on the Arizona equivalent of the Texas Rangers, set in 1903. Murders lead the Captain to suspect the return of the Shaw gang. Nimoy's role cannot be determined.

TWILIGHT ZONE

12/29/61) "A Quality of Mercy" Nimoy has a small role as a soldier in a platoon commanded by a gung-ho lieutenant (Dean Stockwell) who is determined to capture a group of Japanese soldiers, on a Pacific Island near the end of WW II.

TWO FACES WEST

This Western series starred Charles Bateman in two roles: twin brothers Rick and Ben January, a doctor and a lawman, respectively.

(9/12/61) "Doctor's Orders" Old Mrs. Collins is dying, but wants to see her outlaw son

Johnny (Nimoy) one last time. The doctor agrees to help her, and locates Johnny in the hills. Things get complicated when Sheriff Ben January shows up at the Collins' reunion.

THE UNTOUCHABLES
Eliot Ness (Robert Stack) cleans up crime in Prohibition-era Chicago.

(3/1/62) "Takeover" Nimoy plays Packy, the loyal assistant to Zenko (Luther Adler), Chicago's leading beer bootlegger.

THE VIRGINIAN
Western series starring Doug McClure as Trampas.

(12-25-63) "Man of Violence" Nimoy plays Wismer, who killed a friend of Trampas and is being held at a nearby fort. DeForrest Kelley plays Lt. Belden, an army medic who treats the wounded Wismer. A guide kills Wismer after learning where his gold is hidden in Apache territory; Belden believes that he is responsible for the man's death, and heads into Apache territory, too. Belden, Trampas and the guide must cope with Apaches and unravel the truth while they struggle to survive.

(4/14/65) "Showdown" The Virginian (James Drury) rides into a town to make a cattle deal only to find that the town is overrun by crooked ranchers. Marshall Merle Frome (Michael Ansara) and his younger brother Ben, a deputy, are trying to clean up the area. The Virginian joins them in a final gun battle with the villains; Ben is wounded, but the law triumphs.

(11/17/65) "Show Me a Hero" Nimoy plays Keith Bentley, a young lawyer trying to help his newly-founded town raise funds. Outsiders try to get the town to institute gambling, but Bentley leads the opposition to this scheme as it would undermine the sort of community they want to live in. Later, he is beaten by the crooked outsiders, who burn down his house and promise to do the same to the town if it does not go along with them. The Virginian helps Bentley and the townspeople fight off the interlopers, and the townspeople rebuild Bentley's house.

WAGON TRAIN
Western drama focusing on various people headed West.

(10/21/59) "The Estaban Zamora Story" Nimoy plays a young Mexican rancher who unknowingly kills his brother; Ernest Borgnine plays their father.

(4/6/60) "The Maggie Hamilton Story" Nimoy plays a drunken Indian scout in this story about a spoiled young Eastern woman whose immaturity causes troubles on the way West.

(3/22/61) "The Tiburcio Mendez Story" Nimoy plays a judge.

(3/21/62) "The Baylor Crowfoot Story"

THE WEST POINT STORY (CBS/ABC)
(a.k.a. THE MEN OF WEST POINT)
Stories about West Point cadets, based on actual files.

(11/16/56) "His Brother's Fists" Nimoy plays Tom Kennedy, a young man with a knack for boxing but little enthusiasm for a professional career. Instead, he attends West Point. His older brother tells another cadet about Tom's unwillingness to fight, and Tom winds up being leveraged into boxing again, unaware of his brother's manipulations.

(4/12/57) "Cold Peril" Cadet Roy Rupple (Nimoy?) breaks regulations and walks across the frozen Hudson River to visit his girlfriend. His friends learn that an icebreaker is clearing the river, and they try to get him back in time— only to wind up stranded themselves.

Leonard Nimoy appeared in the "Kiss Me Again, Stranger" segment of the THREE FACES OF LOVE TV movie anthology

Star Trek Episode Guide

First Season
1. "The Man Trap" (9/8/66)
Script by G.C. Johnson
A salt vampire impersonates Dr. McCoy's long-lost love.

2. "Charlie X" (9/15/66)
Script by D.C. Fontana & Gene Roddenberry
Charlie is a teenager with great mental powers and a childish personality.

3. "Where No Man Has Gone Before" (9/22/66)
Script by Samuel A. Peeples
The show's second pilot. A crewmember begins to develop godlike powers and presumptions.

4. "The Naked Time" (9/29/66)
Script by John D.F. Black
A deadly disease unlocks the inner secrets of the Enterprise crew. . . including Spock, who cries over his suppressed emotions.

5. "The Enemy Within" (10/6/66)
Script by Richard Matheson
A transporter malfunction splits Kirk into two opposed personalities. First use of the Vulcam neck pinch.

6. "Mudd's Women" (10/13/66)
Script by Roddenberry & Stephen Kandel
Introducing Harry Mudd and his three beautiful companions.

7. "What Are Little Girls Made Of?" (10/20/66)
Script by Robert Bloch
Something's not quite right with an arachaeologist rescued by the Enterprise.

8. "Miri" (10/27/66)
Script by Adrian Spies
Concerning a planet where children retain their youth— up to a point.

9. "Dagger of the Mind" (11/3/66)
Script by S. Bar David (Simon Wincelberg)
Kirk and Spock uncover dark secrets at a supposedly "humane" penal colony.
First use of the Vulcan mind meld.

10. "The Corbomite Maneuver" (11/10/66)
Script by Jerry Sohl
The Enterprise encounters a huge alien ship which intends to destroy it.

11. "The Menagerie", Part One (11/17/66)
Script by Gene Roddenberry
In a story utilizing footage from the first Star Trek pilot, Spock kidnaps the Enterprise's first captain, commandeers the ship, and turns himself in for court martial.

12. "The Menagerie", Part Two (11/24/66)
The story concludes as Spock explains his strange actions.

13. "The Conscience of the King" (12/8/66)
Script by Barry Trivers
Kirk tries to learn if one of his passengers is the man responsible for the murder of thousands.

14. "Balance of Terror" (12/15/66)
Script by Paul Schneider
The Enterprise encounters Romulans, whose leader looks remarkably like Spock's dad.

15. "Shore Leave" (12/29/66)
Script by Theodore Sturgeon
The crew visits a planet where reality goes haywire.

16. "The Galileo Seven" (1/5/67)
Script by Oliver Crawford and S. Bar David
Spock's in charge of a shuttlecraft that crashes on a dangerous planet; he must decide how he and his crew are to survive this ordeal.

17. "The Squire of Gothos" (1/12/67)
Script by Paul Schneider
Kirk & crew become playthings for the seemingly omnipotent Trelane.

18. "Arena"
Script by Gene L. Coon, from Fredric Brown's classic story
Kirk must fight a giant lizard for the fate of human civilization.

19. "Tomorrow Is Yesterday" (1/26/67)
Script by D.C. Fontana
The Enterprise winds up in the 20th century and must erase all evidence of their passing *and* find away back to its proper time.

20. "Court Martial" (2/2/67)
Script by Don M. Mankiewics & S. Carabatsos
The ship's computer is the prime witness against Kirk in a trial for negligence.

21. "The Return of the Archons" (2/9/67)
Script by Gene Roddenberry and Boris Sobelman
Kirk searches for a missing starship crew on a planet where outsiders must assimilate or die.

22. "Space Seed" (2/16/67)
Script by Gene L. Coon and Carel Wilbur
Khan takes over the Enterprise; he is defeated, but Kirk's kidding himself if he thinks he's seen the last of this villain.

23. "A Taste of Armageddon" (2/23/67)
Script by Robert Hammer and Gene L. Coon
Another screwy planet, where wars are waged by computer— and the "casualties" must turn themselves in for euthanasia.

24. "This Side of Paradise" (3/2/67)
Script by Nathan Butler & D.C. Fontana
Kirk loses his crew to a world where airborne spores create a sense of perfect bliss.

25. "The Devil In The Dark" (3/9/67)
Script by Gene L. Coon
Bit of a bother with a silicon monster, until Spock finds out she's just an overprotective mother, courtesy of the Vulcan mind-meld.

26. "Errand of Mercy" (3/23/67)
Script by Gene L. Coon
A bunch of planetary hicks refuse to help Kirk defend their world against Klingons. . . but things are seldom what they seem.

27. "The Alternative" (3/30/67)
Script by Don Ingalls
The universe is in serious trouble when a man battles his anti-matter alter ego and drags the Enterprise into the conflict.

28. "The City On The Edge Of Forever" (4/6/67)
Script by Harlan Ellison (Hugo Award for script)
Kirk and Spock must follow a drug-crazed McCoy through a time portal to prevent history from changing.

29. "Operation: Annihilate" (4/13/67)
Script by Stephen Carabatsos
Giant flying viruses attack people and drive them crazy with pain. Kirk and crew must figure something out or risk being breakfast for these renegade fried eggs.

Second Season
30. "Amok Time" (9/15/67)
Script by Theodore Sturgeon
The classic Spock story, as the mating urge gets the better of the stoic Vulcan and drives him back to his home planet looking for some action.

31. "Who Mourns For Adonis?" (9/22/67)
Script by Gilbert Ralston and Gene L. Coon
The Greek god Apollo makes trouble for Kirk. Go figure.

32. "The Changeling" (9/29/67)
Script by John Meredyth Lucas
The Enterprise encounters NOMAD, an ancient probe bent upon wiping out all biological pests, such as human beings. The first use of this now-familiar idea.

33. "Mirror, Mirror" (10/6/67)
Script by Jerome Bixby
Another transporter foul-up casts Kirk into an alternate universe where the Enterprise is run by a bloodthirsty crew with familiar faces— including a bearded Mr. Spock.

34. "The Apple" (10/13/67)
Script by Max Erlich
A godlike machine provides its subjects a paradise; Kirk and crew run afoul of this being, and troubles ensue.

35. "The Doomsday Machine" (10/20/67)
Script by Norman Spinrad
It's eating planets, and the Enterprise crew just doesn't know what to do about it.

36. "Catspaw" (10/27/67)
Script by Robert Bloch
A spooky Halloween episode, replete with cats and witches.

37. "I, Mudd" (11/3/67)
Script by Stephen Kandel
Mudd's back, prisoner of a planet of androids, and he has no qualms against recruiting some old friends to keep him company.

38. "Metamorphosis" (11/10/67)
Script by Gene L. Coon
An alien in love with a stranded human shanghais the Enterprise to provide companions for its friend.

39. "Journey To Babel" (11/17/67)
Script by D.C. Fontana
Diplomatic intrigue on the Enterprise provides the background for Spock's reunion with his parents.

40. "Friday's Child" (12/1/67)
Script by D.C. Fontana
Kirk tries to save a pregnant woman from execution on a barbaric planet and gets caught up in yet another brouhaha.

41. "The Deadly Years" (12/8/67)
Script by David P. Harmon
An aging disease affects every member of a landing crew except Chekhov. Great Kirk-goes-senile episode. Spock gets off easy since Vulcans age more slowly.

42. "Obsession" (12/15/67)
Script by Art Wallace
Kirk goes after a blood-eating gas monster that got away from him 12 years earlier.

43. "Wolf in the Fold" (12/22/67)
Script by Robert Bloch
On a peaceful planet, an amnesia-struck Scotty is accused of being a vicious killer.

44. "The Trouble With Tribbles" (12/29/67)
Script by David Gerrold
Amusing story about bothersome hairballs. Some (including Mr. Gerrold) count this one as a classic.

45. "The Gamesters of Triskelion" (1/5/68)
Script by Margaret Armen
Kirk, Uhura and Chekhov are kidnapped and forced to become gladiators.

46. "A Piece of the Action" (1/12/68)
Script by David Harmon and Gene L. Coon
Kirk and crew must learn to blend in when they land in a culture patterned after the crime bosses of Depression Chicago. Spock gets nicknamed "Spocko" and wears pinstripes and a fedora.

47. "The Immunity Syndrome" (1/19/68)
Script by Robert Sabaroff
Another doomsday machine plot, this time starring a giant space amoeba. The Enterprise must act as an antibody in order to save the day.

48. "A Private Little War" (2/2/68)
Script by Judd Crucis and G. Roddenberry
Klingons provide weapons to a developing society, so Kirk sets things straight by giving weapons to the other side!

49. "Return To Tomorrow" (2/9/68)
Script by John Kingsbridge
Kirk, Spock and a guest star lend their bodies to some disembodied entities until android hosts can be built— but the being in Spock's body proves to be a lousy tenant who resists eviction.

50. "Patterns of Force" (2/16/68)
Script by John Meredyth Lucas
Kirk tries to stop a planet from recreating Hitler's Third Reich, but it isn't going to be easy.

51. "By Any Other Name" (2/23/68)
Script by Jerome Bixby & D.C. Fontana
The Enterprise is "borrowed" by aliens headed for home; they'll be done with it in 300 years. Kirk is not amused.

52. "Omega Glory" (3/1/68)
Script by Gene Roddenberry
Kirk finds yet another planet suffering from the Roddenberry Syndrome, which causes it to possess a history remarkably similar to Earth's, at one period or another. Here, they seem to be fighting the Vietnam War all over again, but this time it's lasted centuries.

53. "The Ultimate Computer" (3/8/68)
Script by Lawrence Wolfe & D.C. Fontana
A new computer kicks Kirk out of his job and makes life miserable for the good Captain.

54. "Bread and Circuses" (3/15/68)
Script by John Kneubel, Roddenberry & Coon
Roddenberry Syndrome alert! On this planet, the Roman Empire has lasted into the 20th Century, and developed a commensurate technology (cars, TV, etc.). . . but they're still savage and brutal.

55. "Assignment: Earth" (3/29/68)
Script by Art Wallace and Gene Roddenberry
This time, the earth-like planet is Earth, and Teri Garr lives there so it's all right. Kirk goes back to the '60s and runs into Gary Seven, a alien good guy who never got his own series. Spock wears a hat over his ears and looks cool.

Third Season
56. "Spock's Brain" (9/20/68)
Script by Lee Cronin
The lowest point of Spock's career. The organ in question is hijacked by aliens, with Kirk in hot pursuit. Luckily, McCoy is good at putting the things back in.

57. "The Enterprise Incident" (9/27/68)
A Romulan femme fatale captures the Enterprise, incarcerates Kirk and pitches some woo at Spock, who doesn't protest very much. First and last use of the Vulcan Death Grip.

58. "The Paradise Syndrome" (10/4/68)
Script by Margaret Armen
Kirk is stranded with amnesia on a planet inhabited by American Indian types (even though Roddenberry didn't write this episode) and finds true love at last.

59. "And The Children Shall Lead" (10/11/68)
Script by Edward J. Lasko
A famous lawyer plays an evil entity that controls the minds of five children.

60. "Is There In Truth No Beauty?" (10/18/68)
Script by Jean Lisette Aroests
A beautiful human woman is the escort for an alien ambassador who is so ugly no one can look at him without going completely insane. Spock performs a mind-meld but forgets to put his special shades back on when he's done, bringing him face-to-face with the hideous being.

61. "Spectre of the Gun" (10/25/68)
Script by Lee Cronin
Powerful aliens become annoyed with Kirk and send him and his officers to the shootout at the O.K. Corrall— as the losing side.

62. "Day of the Dove" (11/1/68)
Script by Jerome Bixby
An alien blob with a taste for violence drops some very unhappy Klingons on the Enterprise, gives everyone swords, and kicks back for some entertainment.

63. "For The World Is Hollow And I Have Touched The Sky" (11/8/68)
Script by Rick Vollaerts
McCoy, convinced that he's dying, finds romance with the high priestess of a doomed world.

64. "The Tholian Web" (11/15/68)
Script by Judy Barnes and Chet Richards
Kirk slips into space limbo, and territorial-minded aliens hamper Spock's attempts at rescue.

65. "Plato's Stepchildren" (11/22/68)
Script by Meyer Dolinsky
A decadent race of telekinetic sadists make trouble for Kirk and crew, but they need Dr. McCoy's help.

66. "Wink of An Eye" (11/29/68)
Script by Arthur Neineman and Lee Cronin
Aliens who live at an accelerated rate use crew members as host bodies— but the bodies tend to burn out in no time at all.

67. "The Empath" (12/6/68)
Aliens torture Kirk while a strange, empathic mute girl suffers along with him and his officers.

68. "Elaan of Troyius" (12/20/68)
Script by John Meredyth Lucas
Kirk falls for the chemical wiles of a beautiful but annoying high priestess. Her name's similarity to that of an ancient Earth personage is, of course, a complete coincidence.

69. "Whom Gods Destroy" (1/3/69)
Script by Lee Erwin and Jerry Sohl
Inmates at a space prison revolt, and Kirk and Spock must thwart their crazy leader, who, crazy or not, can assume any appearance he chooses. Worth watching for Yvonne Craig (Batgirl).

70. "Let That Be Your Last Battlefield" (1/10/69)
Script by Lee Cronin and Jud Taylor
Two aliens slug it out on the Enterprise. They're both black on one side and white on the other, but they're enemies because they are mirror images of each other, not identical. This episode might be a subtle parable about the pointlessness of racial intolerance. Maybe.

71. "The Mark of Gideon" (1/17/69)
Script by George Slavin and Stanley Adams
Another crazy transporter problem. The crew thinks Kirk has vanished in transit. Kirk thinks he's still on the bridge, but the crew has vanished. Reality will play these tricks from time to time. . .

72. "That Which Survives" (1/24/69)
Script by D.C. Fontana & J.M. Lucas
An encounter with a beautiful woman whose slightest touch is fatal.

73. "The Lights of Zetar" (1/31/69)
Script by Shari Lewis and Jerry Tarcher
Another disembodied alien force attacks people's brains.

74. "Requiem for Methuselah" (2/14/69)
Script by Jerome Bixby
He's real old, he used to live on Earth, and anybody who ever did

anything really important in Earth history was probably really him. Honest.

75. "The Way To Eden" (2/21/69)
Script by Michael Richards and Arthur Heineman
Space hippies stage a sit-in on the Enterprise; Chekov tries to grok but he's too square.

76. "The Cloud Minders" (2/28/69)
Script by Oliver Drawford, Margaret Armen & David Gerrold
On a planet where society is stratified by where people live— in the sky or on the ground— Kirk and Spock must try to obtain some xenite without getting too embroiled in local politics.

77. "The Savage Curtain" (3/7/69)
Script by Gene Roddenberry and Arthur Heinemann
Abraham Lincoln (or a reasonable facsimile thereof) helps Kirk and Spock battle some historical villains, including Genghis Khan.

78. "All Our Yesterdays" (3/14/69)
Script by Jean Lisette Aroeste
A time portal sends the officers to different periods of a doomed planet's past: Kirk is charged with witchcraft in a medieval setting, while Spock, cast back to prehistoric times, becomes illogical and gets involved with Mariette Hartley while McCoy tries to slap some sense into him.

79. "Turnabout Incident" (6/3/69)
Script by Gene Roddenberry and Arthur Heinemann
A woman scientist swaps bodies with Kirk and takes over the ship. Will anyone notice that the Captain is acting a bit differently than usual?

STAR TREK: THE NEXT GENERATION (11/91)
Two-part episode in which Nimoy guest stars as Ambassadore Spock, having at long last continued in his father, Sarek's, footsteps.

Mission Impossible Appearances

Fourth Season
Episode #81: "The Code" (First broadcast 9/28/69)
Paris poses as a El Lider, a South American revolutionary.

#82: "The Numbers Game" (10/5/69)
Paris plays a scar-faced soldier who kills his commander.

#83 & #84: "The Controllers" (Part 1 & 2) (10/12/69 & 10/19/69)
Paris plays a military prosecutor.

#85: "Fool's Gold" (10-29-69)
Paris poses as a counterfeiter.

#86: "Commandants" (11-2-69)
Paris is a Chinese Major.

#87: "Double Circle" (11-9-69)
Plot involves an art collector and the duplication of his apartment.

#88: "Submarine" (11-16-69)
Paris is an "SS" officer.

#89: "The Robot" (11-23-69)
Paris dons an array of disguises: robot, dictator, double, etc.

#90: "Mastermind" (11-30-69)
Paris is Lester Perkins in a "mind-touch" type story.

#91: "The Brothers" (12-7-69)
Paris is Takis Demetrious.

#92: "Time Bomb" (12-14-69)
Paris is a military officer who orders an evacuation.

#93: "The Amnesiac" (12-21-69)
Paris poses as an amnesiac.

#94: "The Falcon" (Part 1) (1-4-70)
Paris is Zastro, the Magician.

#95: "The Falcon" (Part 2) (1-11-70)
Paris is Zastro, the Magician

#96: "The Falcon" (Part 3) (1-18-70)
Paris poses as Prince Nicolai.

#97: "Chico" (1-25-70)
Paris is an Australian sailor.

#98 "Gitano" (2-1-70)
Paris poses as a gypsy.

#99 "Phantoms" (2-8-70)
Luther Adler plays a megalomaniac dictator.

#100 "Terror" (2-15-70)
Paris poses as an Arab military officer.

#101 "Lover's Knot" (2-22-70)
Paris and Phelps form a romantic triangle with Lady Weston.

#102 "Orpheus" (3-1-70)
Paris has an electric ring that allows him to fool a lie detector.

#103 "The Crane" (3-8-70)
Paris poses as a blind man.

#104 "Death Squad" (3-15-70)
Paris pretends to be drunk to discover information.

#105 "The Choice" (3-22-70)
Paris portrays the dual role of a mystic and actor.

#106 "The Martyr" (3-29-70)
Paris poses as the long-lost son of a martyred democratic leader.

Fifth Season
#107 "The Killer" (9-19-70)
Paris is a cab driver.

#108 "Flip Side" (9-26-70)
Paris looks for a break in the music business.

#109 "The Innocent" (10-3-70)
Paris acts as a narcotics agent.

#110 "Homecoming" (10-10-70)
Paris plays Dana's jealous boyfriend.

#111 "The Flight" (10-17-70)
Paris is Marcos, one of the criminals.

#112 "My Friend, My Enemy" (10-24-70)
Paris is captured by enemy agents.

#113 "Butterfly" (10-31-70)
Paris poses as a Kabuki dancer.

#114 "Decoy" (11-7-70)
Phelps assists a lady's defection.

#115 "The Amateur" (11-14-70)
Paris and Barney pose as bicycle racers.

#116 "Hunted" (11-21-70)
Paris acts as a decoy to help rescue Barney.

#117 "The Rebel" (11-28-70)
Paris tricks Bakram and the IMF escape in a hollow statue.

#118 "Squeeze Play" (12-12-70)
Paris poses as an underworld big shot.

#119 "The Hostage" (12-19-70)
Paris poses as an influential "American industrialist."

#120 "Takeover" (1-2-71)
Paris brings the mayor his daughter.

#121 "Cat's Paw" (1-9-71)
Barney helps unmask a crusading editor's killer.

#122 "The Missile" (1-16-71)
Paris and Barney track down a kidnapper.

#123 "The Field" (1-23-71)
Paris poses as a mind field expert.

#124 "Blast" (1-30-71)
Paris poses as the owner of a large show dog.

#125 "The Cataflaque (2-6-71)
Paris is an old man.

#126 "Kitara" (aka **"The Bigot"**) (2-20-71)
Paris is a person of mixed blood in this Africa story.

#127 "A Ghost Story" (2-27-71)
The IMF puzzle over the secret of a deadly nerve gas.

#128 "The Party" (3-6-71)
Paris poses as a Russian.

#129 "The Merchant" (3-27-71)
Paris is a clever card player.

In Search Of . . .

A COMPLETE EPISODE GUIDE
(1976-1982)

First Season
Episode #1: "Loch Ness"
A report on the possible existence of the Loch Ness Monster.

#2: "The Bermuda Triangle"
Are beings from space behind the disappearances in the Bermuda Triangle?

#3: "Ghosts"
Recent studies indicate that there may be reason to take ghosts more seriously.

#4: "UFO's"
Interviews with people who claim to have sighted UFOs.

#5: "Atlantis"
Scenes of structure thought to be Atlantis are examined in the Bahamas.

#6: "Voodoo"
Voodoo practices in Haiti are explored.

#7: "Inca Treasure"
The excavation of a long
forgotten city in Vicabamba.

#8: "Life After Death"
interviews with people who were revived after being clinically dead.

#9: "Dracula"
Exploration of the Rumanian Count rumored to be the "original" Count Dracula.

#10: "Amelia Earhart"
What was the fate of aviation pioneer Amelia Earhart?

#11: "Easter Island Massacres"
A visit to the great stone gods of Easter Island.

#12: "Other Voice"
The sensitivity of plants his studied.

#13: "Earthquakes"
Earthquake prediction techniques are explored.

#14: Strange Visitors"
New Hampshire inscriptions offer evidence that Mediterranean settlers predated Columbus' visit.

#15: "Ancient Flight (Ancient Aviators)"
Indications that beings from other planets visited the earth in ancient times.

#16: "Calls From Space"
Interplanetary communication is investigated.

#17: "Nazi Plunder"
An examination of the continuing search for gold bullion, currency and artistic masterpieces which disappeared with the fall of Nazi Germany.

#18: "The Magic of Stonehenge"
The mysteries of a circular arrangement of prehistoric megaliths in southwestern England.

#19: "Learning ESP"
A study of extra
sensory perception.

#20: "Big Foot"
An investigation of the existence of Bigfoot.

#21: "Mummy's Curse"
An investigation of the unexplained deaths of 30 expedition members in 1922.
#22: "Killer Bees"
Swarms of killer bees are examined.

#23: "Psychic Detectives"
How to solve a murder and give profitable stock investment advice through psychic means.

#24: "Martians"
Theories that Martians had to leave their planet and subsequently migrated to earth in ancient times.

Second Season
#25: "Butch Cassidy"
Did Butch live to a ripe old age in Utah?

#26: "Swamp Monsters"
The alleged existence of a large manlike beast in Honey Island Swamp in Louisiana.

#27: "Secrets of Life (DNA)"
The mysteries of heredity, and the controversial efforts of science to penetrate the DNA molecule.

#28: "Michael Rockefeller"
The disappearance of multimillionaire Michael Rockefeller during an expedition to New Guinea.

#29: "Reincarnation"
Does life end with death or do we merely shed one body for another?

#30: "Witch Doctors in America"
Why are with doctors practicing today in American mental hospitals?

#31: "Haunted Castles"
An exploration of alleged ghost haunts in Great Britain.

#32: "Garden of Eden"
The search for the facts behind the biblical story.

#33: "Deadly Ants"
Ants immune to pest control chemicals.

#34: "The Coming Ice Age"
The weather and speculation concerning the meaning of various climatic change.

#35: "Pyramid Secrets"
The great pyramids of Egypt.

#36: "Mayan Mysteries"
Ruins in Central America of an ancient civilization.

#37: "The Man Who Would Not Die"
A legend persists of a man who lives from age to age assisting mortal men in the perfection of civilization.

#38: "Lost Dutchman Mine"
A treasure of gold is reportedly stashed in Arizona's Superstition Mountains.

#39: "Firewalkers"
In the Spanish village of San Pedro Monrique, the religious practice of firewalking is maintained.

#40: "Astrology"
Astrology and its application to science and business.

#41: "Troy"
The 19th century German archaeologist Heinrich Schleimann's search for the city of Troy.

#42: "Dead Sea Scrolls"
Found in a cave near the Dead Sea were manuscripts concerning a type of Judaism.

#43: "Immortality"
Can advanced science prolong life?

#44: "Hurricanes"
A study in the destructiveness of hurricanes.

#45: "Anastasia"
Speculation that the youngest daughter of Russian czar Nicholas II survived the 1918 slaughter of czar and his family.

#46: "Shark Worshippers"
A cult in the Solomon Islands who love to hang out with their friends, the sharks.

#47: "Hypnosis"
The ancient art which is also becoming a modern tool in science, medicine and criminology.

**#48: "Ogo
Pogo Monster"**
Is there a creature living in the Okanagan Lake in Western Canada? The local Indians believe so.

Third Season
#49: "U.F.O. Captives"
Are aliens kidnapping humans to have their way with them?

#50: "Tornadoes"
Can they be predicted? Can they be stopped? What is the nature of a tornado's awesome, deadly power?

#51: "Cloning"
Will science one day be able to create physical and genetic duplicates of human beings?

#52: "Dowsing (Water Seekers)"
Can a 'divining rod' really find water?

#53: "Jack the Ripper"
Was Jack the Ripper a member of the British royal family?

#54: "Cryogenics"
Can human 'corpsicles' be brought back to life in some future age?

#55: "Money Pit Mystery"
Is Captain Kidd's treasure buried in a mysterious water
filled pit on Oak Island in Canada? Six people have died trying to find out.

#56: "Sodom and Gomorrah"
Did Sodom and Gomorrah really exist and where were they located?

#57: "Great Lakes Triangle"
In the Great Lakes there is an area where there have been more disappearances than in the famed Bermuda Triangle.

#58: "Monster Hunters (Sasquatch)"
Let's take another look at Bigfoot.

#59: "The Siberian Fireball"
On June 30, 1908, something flattened a large area in Siberia which seemingly fell from the sky. What was it?

#60: "King Tut (Tutankhaman)"
What was the story behind the death of the ancient boy king? Was he murdered by jealous priests?

#61: "Bermuda Triangle Pirates"
Could modern day pirates be pillaging and sinking boats in the Bermuda Triangle?

#62: "Mayan Legacy"
A look an the culture of the Mayan's in Mexico and Central America and what kind of technology they seemed to possess.

#63: "Sherlock Holmes"
Various sources for the Sherlock Holmes character are examined.

#64: "Lost Vikings"
Theories concerning the disappearance of the Viking colony in Greenland.

#65: "Dreams and Nightmares"
An inquiry into the nature of dreams and nightmares.

#66: "Animal ESP"
Do animals have ESP?

#67: "Psychic Seahunt"
Can a psychic "visualize" the location of shipwrecks?

#68: "The Angel of Death"
A Nazi
hunter stalks Dr. Josef Mengele.

#69: "Noah's Flood"
A look a a variety of flood myths.

#70: "The Diamond Curse"
A look at the "curses" behind several famous gems.

#71: "Ghostly Stakeout"
Troubled spirits and ghosts cling to their former environments.

#72: "Brain Power"
The hidden untapped potential of the human brain.

Fourth Season
#73: "The Amityville Horror"
A "possessed" house in New York.

#74: "Tidal Waves"
A look at these underwater disturbances.

#75: "Carlos: The World's Most Wanted Man"
A look at a world terrorist.

#76: "Pompeii"
A volcano destroys the small Roman city in 79 A.D.

#77: "The Abominable Snowman"
The Sherpa natives discuss this creature's existence.

#78: "Immortal Sharks"
A look at the Great White Shark.

#79: "D.B. Cooper"
What happened to the man who parachuted from a plane with $200,000 in cash?

#80: "The Shroud of Turin"
Did this shroud cover the body of Jesus Christ?

#81: "Australian UFOs"
Why are more UFO sightings over the Southern Hemisphere?

#82: "The Lost Colony of Roanoke"
What happened to a colony of 112 settlers in North Carolina?

#83: "Wild Children"
A look at children raised by animals.

#84: "Mexican Pyramids"
Pyramids in the rain forests of Mexico and Guatemala.

#85: "The Ghost Ship"
The *Mary Celeste* is found abandoned in 1881.

#86: "The Dark Star"
Tribal worship of an ancient star.

#87: "The Ten Commandments"
A look at Sinai and the Mountain of Moses.

#88: "The Missing Heir"
A look at an unclaimed stock certificate for 3.2 million dollars.

#89: "The Bimini Wall"
Do the remains of Atlantis lie submerged off the shore of Bimini?

#90: "Vincent Van Gogh"
Was Van Gogh an epileptic?

#91: "The San Andreas Fault"
A look at one of the longest and most dangerous earthquake zones in the world.

#92: "John The Baptist"
Were the bones of John the Baptist smuggled out of the Holy Land to be kept safe in the Egyptian desert?

#93: "Past Lives"
Can reincarnation be proven?

#94: "Earth Visitors"
Is human life the product of inbreeding by space travelers?

#95: "Air Disaster Predictions"
A study of vivid, recurring nightmares that forewarn of major air disasters.

#96: "Glenn Miller"
Why was Glenn Miller's death never investigated and why was no search ever made of the plane.
Fifth Season
#97: "UFO Coverups"
Is the Air Force suppressing vital information concerning UFO sightings and landings?

#98: "Faith Healing"
Can we tap mental forces that trigger healing?

#99: "Lee Harvey Oswald"
Were there two assassins of J.F.K.?

#100: "The Daredevil Deathwish"
A look at a daredevil's wish to cheat fate.

#101: "Life after Life"
A look at out of body experiences surrounding death.

#102: "Moon Madness"
Do the cycles of the moon trigger mental imbalances?

#103: "The Fountain of Youth"
Can modern science retard aging?

#104: "Dangerous Volcanoes"
Can we predict their eruption?

#105: "The Lindbergh Kidnapping"
Was the arrested man framed?

#106: "Acupuncture"
Does it work?

#107: "Jimmy Hoffa"
What were the facts behind his disappearance?

#108: "Laugh Therapy"
Does laughter keep one healthy?

#109: "Salem Witches"
A look at the some of the lives of 400 witches living in Salem.

#110: "Sun Worshippers"
Solar power is explored.

#111: "Super Children"
Child prodigies and geniuses.

#112: "The Great Wall of China"
A look at this monumental construction.

#113: "The Lusitania"
The facts behind the sinking of this ship.

 # 114: "End of the World"
How and when will the end of the world occur?

#115: "The Holy Grail"
Did the silver chalice ever exist?

#116: "The Death of Marilyn Monroe"
Or was it murder?

#117: "The Hindenburg Mystery"
Was it destroyed by political sabotage?

#118: "Chinese Explorers"
Did the Chinese discover America more than 1000 years before Columbus?

#119: "Castle of Secrets"
A look at the "Coral Castle" near Miami.

#120: "Great Lovers"
The life and times of Don Juan and Casanova.

#121: "M.I.A.s"
Where are the 2,528 soldiers unaccounted for?

#122: "Biofeedback"
Patients monitoring their own internal functions.

#123: "Jesse James"
Did Jesse arrange his own funeral as an escape ruse?

#124: "The Human Aura"
Kirlian photography and auras.

#125: "Ghosts in Photography"
What is the nature of ghostly images in photographs.

#126: "Tower of London Murders"
Two boy kings disappear without a trace, leaving the throne to Richard the 3rd.

#127: "Jim Jones"
Explorations into the mass suicide in Guayana.

#128: "The Elephant Man"
The life of the brutally deformed John Merrick.

#129: "Time and Space Travel"
How many people through the ages have been captivated by the thought of time travel?

#130: "Houdini's Secrets"
The man's life and untimely death are explored.

#131: "The Lincoln Conspiracy"
Did Booth act with cohorts?

#132: "The Missing Link"
Darwin's theory is explored.

#133: "King Solomon's Mines"
The hunt for the secret source of this fabled wealth.

#134: "The Aztec Conquest"
The defeat of the Aztecs by Hernan Cortes.

#135: "Nostradamus"
The French physician's uncanny prophecies.

#136: "Future Life"
What utopian life does the future store?

#137: "The Titanic"
A look at the sinking of this unsinkable vessel.

#138: "Hiroshima Survivors"
The aftermath of a nuclear explosion.

#139: "The Ultimate Disaster"
The aftermath of the Mt. St. Helens Explosion and other natural disasters.

#140: "Eva Braun"
Who was the woman behind Adolf Hitler, and what was the nature of their strange bond?

#141: "Life Before Birth"
Is the infant aware of mother's activities? Capable of thought, emotion and memory?

#142: "The Walls of Jericho"
A look at the biblical story.

#143: "Bishop Pike"
Was he a martyr or a madman?

#144: "Spirit Voices"
Is it possible to break through to the barrier of the beyond?

Motion Pictures

This appendix lists both theatrically released films and feature-length television movies in which Leonard Nimoy appeared as an actor and/or directed.

1951

QUEEN FOR A DAY [HIGH DIVER] Released 3/14/51

Running time: 107 minutes

A United Artists release, in black and white

PRODUCTION CREDITS: Producer: Robert Stillman; Associate producer: Seton I. Miller; Director: Arthur Lubin; Screenplay: Seton I. Miller; Original story: John Ashworth; Music: Hugo Friedhofer; Musical director: Emil Neumann; Director of Photography: Guy Roe, A.S.C.; Art Director: Peggy Fergusson; Film Editor: George Amy, A.C.E.; Production manager: Charles Kerr; Assistant director: Ivan Volkman; Dialogue director: Jus Aldiss; Sound: Jean Speak; Set Decorator: Edward G. Boyle; Makeup artist: Louis Phillipi; Casting Director: Russell Trost; Production Assistant: John Stillman, Jr.; Hair Stylist: Louise Michle; Wardrobe: Josheph King & Ann Peck; Technical: Charles Rose & Morris Rosen; Properties: Irving Sindler; Script supervisor: Arnold Laven

CAST: Stanley Nalawak: Adam Williams; Mrs. Nalawak: Kasia Orzazewski; Mr. Nalawak: Albert Ben-Astar; Peggy: Tracy Roberts; Deacon McAllister: Larry Johns; Daredevil Rinaldi: Grace Lenard; **Chief Kojouski: Leonard Nimoy** (misspelled "Nemoy" in credits); Satchelbutt: Danny Davenport; Mrs. Kimpel: Madge Blake

In this, one of three segments of the film, Leonard Nimoy has the supporting role of "Chief" Kojouski, a young football-playing buddy of the main character, Stanley (Adam Williams). Stanley and his friends are already out of high school but seem to have no choices beyond staying in their small town and working at the mill like their immigrant fathers before them. Stan decides to take a long shot and accepts a job as a high diver with a travelling carnival, even though the job is highly dangerous, and his parents don't approve. Stan spends a last evening in town at the carnival with "Chief" and other friends, and ultimately performs his first— and last— stunt jump. When he emerges from the tank, bruised but in one piece after his 110-foot dive, he discovers that his mother has won a college scholarship for him by appearing on the television program "Queen For A Day." (Presumably, the other two stories in this film also hinged on similar happy endings.) "Chief" and the others congratulate Stan, who now has a ticket to the outside world that doesn't involve risking his neck for a living.

RHUBARB

Released 8/2/51

A Paramount release, in black and white

Running time: 94 minutes

PRODUCTION CREDITS: Producers: William Perlberg and George Seaton; Director: Arthur Lubin; Screenplay: Dorothy Reid and Francis Cockrill; From the novel by H. Allen Smith; Photography: Lionel Lindon; Music: Van Cleave; Editor: Alma Maerorie; Art Directors: Hal Pereira and Henry Bumstead

CAST: Eric Yeager: Ray Milland; Polly: Jan Sterling; T.J. Banner: Gene Lockhart; Myra Banner: Elsie Holmes; P. Duncan Monk: Taylor Holmes; Len Sickles: William Frawley; Orlando Dill: Willard Waterman; Dud Logan: Henry Slate; Doom: James Hayward; First Ballplayer: Anthony Redeckl; **Second Ballplayer: Leonard Nimoy;** Oggie Meadows: James J. Griffith; Additional cast: Strother Martin, Roberta Richards

This movie, starring Ray Milland, is about a tough alley cat named Rhubarb who is the sole beneficiary of an eccentric millionaire's will. The cat's inheritance includes a baseball team, the Brooklyn Loons, who are embarrassed when crowds begin to meow at them. Since they can't break their contracts, all the players feign injuries, but Eric, the will's executor and the team manager's daughters fiancé (Ray Milland) talks them into playing. He does this by convincing them that the cat is a good luck mascot. Eric rigs matters so that once some team members rub the cat, their manager will run in with previously withheld salary. They fall for it, and a character credited only as "Second Ballplayer" (Nimoy) asks if Rhubarb will be at the game.

Eric begrudgingly agrees, and "Second Ballplayer" expresses considerable excitement at this. This is the only scene in which Nimoy has any lines, although he is seen in subsequent scenes as well.

The rest of the story propels the team through a string of victories. Every player pets Rhubarb for luck before going to bat. (How they pick up luck for their defense is not quite explained.) Matters get complicated when a gambling boss kidnaps Rhubarb, but he is located thanks to the fact that Eric's fiancee is allergic to that specific feline. Needless to say, everything works out in the end, and Nimoy and his teammates win the championship.

1952

KID MONK BARONI Released 4/17/52

A Realart release of Jack Broder (Herman Cohen) production

Running time 79 minutes

PRODUCTION CREDITS: Producer: Jack Broder; Associate Producer: Herman Cohen; Director: Harold Schuster; Screenplay: Aben Kandel; Director of Photography: Charles Van Enger; Film Editor: Jason Bernie; Art Director: James Sullivan; Set Decoration: Edward Boyle; Dialogue Director: Charles Maxwell; Musical Composer/ Conductor: Herschel Burke Gilbert; Orchestrations: Joseph Mullendore and Walter Sheets; Additional Dialogue: Richard Conway; Men's Wardrobe: Burell King; Women's Wardrobe: Jeanne Keethe; Hairdresser: Ann Locker; Makeup: Lee Greenway; Script Supervisor: Joan Eremin; Sound: Vic Appel; Leonard Nimoy's Wardrobe: Jim Clinton's; Assistant Director: Ben Chapman

CAST: Father Callahan: Richard Rober; Mr. Hellman: Bruce Cabot; Emily Brooks: Allene Roberts; June, The Counter Gal: Mona Knox; **Paul Baroni: Leonard Nimoy**; Angelo: Jack Larson (a.k.a. Jimmy Olsen!); Mama Baroni: Kathleen Freeman; Knuckles: Budd Jaxon; Pete: Archer MacDonald; Papa Gino Baroni: Joseph Mell; Mr. Petry: Paul Maxey; Mr. Moore: Stuart Randall; Joey: Chad Mallory; Additional Cast: Ted Avery, Madeline Broder, Maurice Cass, Bill Cahanne

This B-picture is a bit of a throwback to the films of a decade earlier, which may account for its present obscurity. It stars Leonard Nimoy as Paul Baroni, a young man in a street gang, who is nicknamed "Monk" because of his deformed face (the facial appliances worn by Nimoy in this role were created by makeup man Lee Greenway, who would provide Mr. Spock with his trademark ears, fifteen years later).

A kindly priest, Father Callahan, attempts to straighten out the kids, and Paul responds to his concern. At the priest's suggestion, he takes up boxing, although only as a sport. He is also introduced to a girl, Emily, who sees past his face to the person within. He even joins the choir, only to be harassed by his former friends in the gang. A fight breaks out, during which Paul accidentally strikes Father Callahan, who is attempting to break up the melée.

Angry at himself, Paul flees the neighborhood and becomes a boxer, since fighting seems to be the only thing he is any good at. At first, he is sponsored by a pawnbroker, and receives nothing more than unredeemed watches as payment for his six consecutive knockouts. He moves into professional circles and begins to make greater sums of money in the ring.

One day, listening to choir music in a record store, he meets Father Callahan, who forgives him, and asks him to attend a church dance, where he meets Emily again. They begin to develop a relationship, and eventually Emily suggests to Paul that he have plastic surgery on his face. He does, only to notice that women who once spurned him now look at him with interest. He starts dating another woman, more glamorous than Emily, and spends more and more money on her until he realizes that he's gone broke. The woman dumps Paul when she discovers this.

He goes back to Emily, but she finds him changed, having become too self-centered and narcissistic. She goes away to teach.

Paul's boxing career falls apart too, as he now is too defensive a fighter to really compete, being too worried about damage to his new face. He eventually disappears into skid row.

His manager locates him and tries to get him to fight again. They try to revive his older, more successful boxing style, after Hellman convinces him to take part in a charity match that will benefit Callahan's church. Paul loses the fight and takes a real pummeling, but even so, the loser's purse goes to the church. Paul and Emily are reunited, and eventually marry.

FRANCIS GOES TO WEST POINT

Released 6/13/52

A Universal-International release, in black and white

Running time: 81 minutes

PRODUCTION CREDITS: Producer: Robert Arthur; Director: Arthur Lubin; Screenplay: David Stern; Photography: Irving Glassberg; Music: David Skinner

CAST: Donald O'Connor, Alice Kelley, Francis the Talking Mule, Leonard Nimoy

This, the third in the inexplicably popular series about a wise-cracking mule and his slow-witted human sidekick (O'Connor) features Leonard Nimoy in a negligible role.

ZOMBIES OF THE STRATOSPHERE

A Republic Serial in 12 chapters

CHAPTER TITLES: 1) The Zombie Vanguard, 2) Battle of the Rockets, 3) Undersea Agents, 4) Contraband Cargo, 5) The Iron Executioner, 6) Murder Mine, 7) Death on the Waterfront, 8) Hostage for Murder, 9) The Human Torpedo, 10) Flying Gas Chamber, 11) Man. vs. Monster, 12) Tomb of the Traitors.

PRODUCTION CREDITS: Screenplay: Ronald Davidson; Associate Producer: Franklin Adreon; Director: Fred C. Brannon; Unit Manager: Roy Wade; Director of Photography: John MacBurnie; Art Director: Fred A. Ritter; Music: Stanley Wilson; Film Editor: Cliff Bell, A.C.E.; Sound: Dick Tyler; Set Decorations: John McCarthy, Jr., James Redd; Special Effects: Howard Lydecker, Theodore Lydecker; Makeup Supervision: Bob Mark; Optical Effects: Consolidated Film Industries

CAST; Larry Martin: Judd Holdren; Sue Davis: Aline Towne; Bob Wilson: Wilson Wood; Marex: Lane Bradford; Harding: Stanley Waxman; Roth: John Crawford; Steele: Craig Kelly; Shane: Ray Boyle; **Narab: Leonard Nimoy;** Truck Driver: Tom Steele; Telegrapher: Dale Van Sickel; Lawson: Roy Engel; Kerr: Jack Harden; Fisherman: Paul Stader; Dick: Gayle Kellogg; Policeman: Jack Shea; Elah: Robert Garabedian; Gomez Operator: Jack Mack; Kettler: Robert Strange; Officer 1: Floyd Criswell; Officer 2: Davison Clark; Pilot: Paul Gustine; Plane Heavy: Henry Rowland; Ross: Clifton Young; Tarner: Norman Willis; Train Heavy 1: George Magrill; Train Heavy 2: Frank Alten; Walker: Tom Steele

A rocket from the planet Mars is detected as it enters the Earth's atmosphere. Larry Martin, an executive in the interplanetary patrol, dons his flying suit and takes off to intercept the spacecraft. The ship lands near some mountains and two aliens, Marex and Narab, emerge to confer with their human conspirators, Roth and Shane. They transfer their shipment to a truck and the spacecraft takes off again just as Larry Martin comes flying over. Knowing that he could not catch the rocket, Larry flies in and lands on the truck. He places a direction-finder on the truck before a low-hanging branch sweeps him off.

The equipment is taken to a cave which has a secret area which can be entered only by climbing down a ladder into an underwater tunnel, and then climbing up another ladder into the secret cave. The Martians are able to do this without the use of any special breathing apparatus. Marex and Narab usually remain in the secret cavern, working on the hydrogen bomb, while Roth and Shane recruit outside help and acquire additional material which the Martians didn't bring with them.

A scientist, Dr. Harding, is contacted by Marex and is persuaded to help in their scheme with grandiose promises of what his life will be like on Mars.

Larry Martin and his assistants, Bob Wilson and Sue Davis, keep on the lookout for the return of the rocket. They also cross the path of the conspirators when they commit daring robberies to obtain their necessary supplies. This includes the robbery of a bank by a robot. Larry manages to track the robot to the cavern where it attacks and almost kills him before Larry pushes it against a huge machine and shortcircuits it. He doesn't realize that close by is a hydrogen bomb which, when exploded, will knock the Earth out of its orbit so that Mars can be moved in and benefit from the better orbit.

Larry takes the robot back to his headquarters, not realizing that it was just temporarily disabled. Dr. Harding uses its remote camera to spy on Larry and then the robot attempts to kill him again. This time when it's defeated, Larry orders that the robot be completely disassembled.

He tries to surrender, but is slain by Marex. The Martians set the bomb to explode in two hours and flee in their spacecraft. But Larry Martin's rocket shoots it down. As Larry approaches the wreck, Narab pulls himself out the door and reveals the location of the bomb to Larry. Martin races to the cavern, swims underwater to the other cave and quickly disables the bomb, saving the Earth.

Although some sources refer to this as Nimoy's first feature film appearance, it's actually his fifth. It is his first role as an alien, though. He is embarrassed by mentions of the film today and when once questioned about it he laughed and replied, "You must forgive me—I needed the money."

The Fifties marked the last hurrah of the movie serial as these films were essentially aimed at children who were already being wooed away by the lure of television and its similar, action-oriented fare. Beginning in the Thirties, Republic made a total of 66 serials. Their last six were made following *Zombies of the Stratosphere*.

The rocket suit worn by Judd Holdren in this serial was established in the late Forties in *King of the Rocketmen,* seen on a different character in the serial *Radar Men From The Moon* and last seen here in *Zombies.* It was also seen in the short-lived *Commando Cody* TV series in 1955 in which Judd Holdren wore both the rocket suit and a mask underneath the helmet.

The robot seen in this serial consists largely (but not entirely) of stock footage from the earlier serial *The Mysterious Dr. Satan.* For instance, the scene in which the robot robs a bank and surprises a guard is lifted entirely from the other serial while the fights with Larry Martin are new footage.

Although Nimoy doesn't have a lot of lines as Narab, his Boston accent is still very pronounced here. Perhaps it's supposed to be a Martian accent?

Although as science fiction films go, this one is pretty obvious, it's colorful and has a lot of action. It's fun to watch and is played so painfully straight as to be positively arch. Watching it one gets the same feeling one gets from watching an Irwin Allen TV show like *Time Tunnel* or *Voyage to the Bottom of the Sea.*

Satan's Satellites is the title of the 70 minute feature version of the serial which was released in 1958. Although serials in the Thirties and early Forties had 20 minute chapters, these started to shorten in the late Forties until by the time *Zombies* was made they averaged 13 minutes a chapter with a 20 minute chapter one. Thus while some sources list the running time of the complete serial at 4 hours, it is actually much closer to 3 hours.

A new re-edited version, complete with chapter titles and cliffhangers, has been Colorimaged and condensed to fit in a two-hour TV time slot. Bearing its original title, *Zombies Of The Stratosphere,* it is being sold in syndication along with other Republic serials and aired in July 1991 On the Family Channel cable network.

1953

THE OLD OVERLAND TRAIL

Released 2/25/53

A Republic Picture, in black and white

PRODUCTION CREDITS: Associate Producer: Edward J. White; Director: William Witney; Script: Milton Raison ; Photography: John MacBurnie; Art Director: Frank Arrigo; Music: R. Dale Butts; Film Editor: Harold Minter, A.C.E.; Assistant Director: Robert

Shannon; Sound: T.A. Carmen; Set Decorations: John McCarthy, Jr. and George Milo; Special Effects: Howard and Theodore Lydecker; Makeup: Bob Mark; Optical Effects: Consolidated Film Industies

CAST: Rex Allen: Rex Allen; The Miracle Horse: Koko; Slim Pickens: Slim Pickens; John Anchor: Roy Barcroft; Mary Peterson: Virginia Hall; Jim Allen: Gil Herman; Draftsman: Wade Crosby; **Apache Chief Black Hawk: Leonard Nimoy;** Mack: Don Murray; Proprietor: Harry Harvey; Joe: Billy Dix; Roger Peterson: Lee Shumway; Pete: Joe Yrigoyen; Sergeant: Marshall Reed; The Republic Rhythm Riders

Rex Allen is sent by the government to put down an Apache uprising. Accompanied by Slim Pickens, the musical group the Rhythm Riders, and his second-billed Miracle Horse, Rex heads West and helps defend a wagon train against Black Hawk (Nimoy) and his warriors. (This is the second and final time that Nimoy has had an animal get higher billing than himself). A typical Western programmer of the period, this movie is justifiably obscure.

1954

THEM!

Released 6/19/1954

A Warner Brothers release, in black and white

PRODUCTION CREDITS: Producer: David Weisbart; Director: Gordon Douglas; Story: George Worthing Yates; Adaptor: Russell Hughes; Screenplay: Ted Sherdemann; Art Director: Stanley Fletcher; Music: Bronislau Kaper; Special Effects: Ralph Ayers; Sound Special Effects: William Mueller and Francis J. Scheid; Photography: Sid Hickox; Editor: Thomas Reilly

CAST: Sergeant Ben Peterson: James Whitmore; Dr. Harold Medford: Edmund Glenn; Dr. Patricia Medford: Joan Weldon; Robert Graham: James Arness; Brigadier General O'Brien: Onslow Stevens; Major Kibbee: Sean McClory; Ed Blackburn: Chris Drake; Little Girl: Sandy Descher; Mrs. Lodge: Mary Ann Hokanson; Captain of Troopers: Don Shelton; Crotty: Fess Parker; Jensen: Olin Howland; Additional cast: Dub Taylor, **Leonard Nimoy**, William Schallert and Ann Doran

America's home-grown giant monster classic, in which humanity must battle against overgrown ants. Nimoy has a walk-on as a soldier; he hands someone some papers and walks back out. He has one line. Don't blink!

1958

SATAN'S SATELLITES

This is the feature version of the 12 chapter **Zombies** serial; see above.

THE BRAIN EATERS

Released Halloween, 1958

An American International Pictures/Corinthian release

PRODUCTION CREDITS: Producer: Edwin Nelson; Director: Bruno VeSota; Story and screenplay: Gordon Urqhart; Associate Producer: Stanley Bickman; Production Manager: Amos Powell; Editor: Carlo Lodato; Assistant Director: Mike Murphy; Makeup: Alan Trumble; Wardrobe: Charles Smith; Photography: Larry Raimond; Art Direction: Burt Shonberg; Sound: James Fullerton; Title design: Robert Balser; Music: Tom Jonson

CAST: Dr. Kettering: Edwin Nelson; Glenn: Alan Frost; Senator Powers: Jack Hill; Alice: Joanna Lee; Elaine: Jody Fair; Dr. Wyler: David Hughes; Dan Walker: Robert Ball; Sheriff: Greigh Phillips; Cameron: Orville Sherman**; Protector: Leonard Nimoy**; Doctor: Doug Banks; Telegrapher: Henry Randolph

Space parasites attach themselves to people's necks and control their brains; Nimoy has a small role.

1963

THE BALCONY

Released 3/21/1963

A BLC/British Lion release, in black and white

Running time: 84 minutes

PRODUCTION CREDITS: Producers: Joseph Strick and Ben Maddow; Director: Joseph Strick; Screenplay by Ben Maddow; Based on the play by Jean Genet, translated by Bernard Frechtman; Director of Photography: George Folsey, A.S.C.; Film Editor: Chester W. Schaeffer; Music: Igor Stravinsky; Conductor: Robert Craft; Art Direction: John Nicholson, Jean Owens, Gabriel Scognamillo; Music Editor: Carl Mahakian; Production Manager: Joel Glickman; Production Associate: Rosemary Kaye; Assistant Director: Helen Levitt; Camera Operator: Frank Dugas; Sound Editors: Verna Fields and Jeanne Turner

CAST: Madame Irma: Shelley Winters; Police Chief: Peter Falk; Carmen: Lee Grant; Thief: Ruby Dee; Judge: Peter Brocco; Bishop: Jeff Corey; Penitent: Joyce Jameson; Horse: Arnette Jens; **Roger: Leonard Nimoy**; General: Kent Smith

Madame Irma (Shelley Winters) operates a thriving brothel that offers refuge from the revolution-torn streets outside. The brothel is actually a converted sound stage where Irma and her associates can create any illusion to cater to their clients. The fantasies indulged in here are all power-oriented: a gas station attendant becomes a Greek Orthodox Bishop hearing confessions, an accountant becomes a Chief Justice dispensing judgements,

and a milkman ascends to the rank of general.

These illusions are dispelled when the Chief of Police (Peter Falk) staggers in, wounded in the riot outside. He forces the three fake dignitaries outside and uses their masquerade to restore order, but strips them of their illusions when their new power starts to go to their heads. Back inside, Irma tries to seduce the Police Chief, only to be interrupted when the rebel leader Roger (Leonard Nimoy), who is defeated, enters. Fending off the women's attempts at seduction, the two men debate the issues surrounding their conflict, only to break into physical violence. Irma's entourage attacks the men, breaking up their fight and stripping them of their clothes. The former enemies leave the brothel, wearing nothing more than bath towels, and walk down the street engaged in friendly a friendly discussion of power.

1965

DEATHWATCH

Premiered 1/20/65

Released 6/27/65

Deathwatch Company, Inc./distributed by Altura Films International

Prints run from 88 to 94 minutes. In black and white.

PRODUCTION CREDITS: Producers: Leonard Nimoy, Vic Morrow; From the play "Haute Surveillance" (Deathwatch) by Jean Genet; Adaptation and Screenplay: Barbara Turner, Vic Morrow; Director of Photography: Vilis Lapenieks; Additional Photography: Joel Coleman; Supervising Editor: Irving Lerner; Film Editor: Verna Fields; Music: Gerald Fried; Production Coordinator: Chase Mitchell; Art Direction: James G. Freiburger; Gaffer: David Stern; Opticals: Modern Film Effects; Assistant Cameraman: Ron McMan-

nus; Sound Recording: G. Barry Atwater; Sound Assistant: Min-
daugus Bagden; Key Grip: Carl Olsen; Script Supervisor: Hannah
Scheel; Co-Editor: Georges Ville; Assistant Editor: Yvonne Mart;
Musical Editor: Peter Zinner; Still Photography: Bernard Abramson;
Music: Tammy Hoffs; Wardrobe: Andre Tayir; Title Design: Block;
THE PRODUCERS THANK WARDEN JACK FOGLIANI, HIS
STAFF AND INMATE MEMBERS OF SYNANON AND AL-
COHOLICS ANONYMOUS AT THE NEVADA STATE PRISON
FOR THEIR COOPERATION.

CAST; **Julian Lefranc: Leonard Nimoy**; Greeneyes: Michael For-
est; Maurice: Paul Mazursky; The Guard: Robert Ellenstein; Street
Girl: Susan Breckir; Emil: Gavin MacLeod; With: Fletcher First,
Robert Pickering, Andre Taylor, Ed Johnson

In a French prison, Jules Lefranc has connived his way into becoming the cellmate of Greeneyes, an important new prisoner and
convicted murderer. Jules was convicted for the armed robbery of a
jewelry store, a comparatively petty offense. Jules idolizes the often
violent Greeneyes and has been taken into the man's confidence.
Greeneyes can neither read nor write and has Jules read his wife's
letters to him and writer back to her for him.

Jules prefers this strange prison environment to the outside world
and feels that his relationship with Greeneyes is threatened by Maurice, the punk whom Greeneyes uses and who caters to his every
whim. Jules fails to perceive that Greeneyes could never truly respect a man like Maurice and is just using him.

In order to hurt Greeneyes, Jules writes the letters to the man's wife
in such a way that she'll know that it isn't Greeneyes himself who is
writing them. Soon she writes back saying that she has realized this
and doesn't want to see him again. Greeneyes is despondent and
sees through what Jules has done. Jules is due to be released soon
and Greeneyes is certain that Jules wanted the woman for himself.

Greeneyes wants his wife killed for turning away from him and
Maurice eagerly agrees to commit the deed when he is released
soon, which further enrages Jules.

In his despondency, Greeneyes reveals how he murdered a girl in
the passion of the moment and without even realizing what he was
doing, believing even after he killed her that he could bring her back
to life. He didn't ask for what has happened to him and wishes it had
never happened.

On visiting day Greeneyes's wife comes to visit with him but they
quarrel even though he was grateful that she came.

Back in the cell Jules momentarily achieves his dream of being accepted by Greeneyes when a tattoo on Jules makes Greeneyes believe that his background is different from what it really is. But Maurice proves that the tattoo is just drawn on and rubs off, shattering Jules' dream.

Depressed and wanting to be accepted by Greeneyes on his level, Jules strangles Maurice so that he'll remain in the cell with Greeneyes. But the other man detests Jules for his act because Maurice meant nothing and by killing him he accomplished nothing. Greeneyes summons the guard who comes and sees what Jules has done.

This is one of those strange, brooding plays in which men thrown together in close quarters reveal who they really are on their basest levels. It is a play created for actors to revel in and it's not surprising that two actors produced the film so that one of them could direct it while the other one stars in it.

While the character of Maurice is introduced in such a way that his mincing is supposed to communicate his homosexuality, that facet of him remains otherwise obliquely dealt with and what rare mentions of it which come up are obscure. Even the reference to him as a "punk" seems obvious until you understand that in prison lingo a "punk" is a passive partner in a homosexual relationship. Jules taunting of Maurice go no further than when he tells him that Greeneyes isn't even thinking about him when he's seeing his wife and would rather be with her.

The illogic of human nature is explored in much of this play, such as when Greeneyes wants his wife killed for leaving him even though he's in prison for murder and will be executed and thus never would have been reunited with his wife in any event. It's as though he doesn't understand why a woman wouldn't want to remain married to a convicted murderer who apparently killed another woman in the heat of a brutal extra-marital affair.

Jules is someone who escapes into his fantasies, such as when he remembers back on the jewelry store heist and how he draped himself with the jewels he was stealing, which surely must have delayed him so that he was captured. His most transcendent moment in life seems to come when Greeneyes accepts him as an equal, which makes the fall engineered by Maurice all the more bitter for him. When Jules is embraced by Greeneyes, we actually feel his joy of success even though it's just the success of someone locked up in a dingy prison cell.

This is an interesting play which translates well into a film where the actors dominate the action with their strong performances.

Paul Mazursky went on to be an actor, and, more importantly, a director, himself.

Michael Forest was reunited with Nimoy a couple years later in the *Star Trek* episode "Who Mourns For Adonis."

1967

VALLEY OF MYSTERY

Originally a 43-minute, unaired, unsold TV pilot ("Stranded"), this was expanded and released theatrically on 4/21/67.

A Universal Picture

94 minutes, Technicolor.

PRODUCTION CREDITS: Executive Producer: (Pilot version only: Frank Price); Producer: Harry Tatelman ; (Original pilot: Frank P. Rosenberg); Director: Joseph Leytes ; (Original pilot: Leon Benson); Screenplay: Richard Neal and Lowell Barrington ; (Pilot version: Dick Nelson); Story: Richard Neal and Lawrence B. Marcus; (Pilot version: Dick Nelson and Lawrence B. Marcus); Director of Photography: Walter Strenge; Color Coordinator: Robert Brower; Art Director: Russel Kimball and Howard E. Johnson; Set Decoration: John McCarthy and John M. Dwyer; Film Editor: Gene Milford; Music: Jack Elliott; Music Supervisor: Stanley Wilson; Sound: Corson Jowett and David H. Moriarity; Assistant Directors: Edward K. Dodds and George Bisk; Unit Production Manager: Abby Singer; Costume: Burton Miller; Makeup: Bud Westmore; Hairstyles: Larry Germain

CAST: Wade Cochran: Richard Egan; Ben Barstow: Peter Graves; Pete Patton: Joby Baker; Rita Brown: Lois Nettleton; Danny O'Neill: Harry Guardino; Joan Simon: Julie Adams; Francisco Rivera: Fernando Lamas; Dr. Weatherly: Alfred Ryder; Connie Lane: Karen Sharpe; Ann Dickson: Barbara Werle; Dino Boretti: Lee Patterson; Manuel Sanchez: Rodolfo Acosta; Charles Kiley: Douglas Kennedy; Jim Walker: Don Stewart; **Spence Atherton: Leonard Nimoy;** Juan Hidalgo: Tony Patino; Dr. John Quincy: Otis Young; Margo York: Lisa Gaye; Forest Hart: George Tyne; Indian Boy: Larry Domasin; M'Tu: Eddie Little Sky; Immigration Inspector: William Phipps

A jetliner crashes in a storm; no one is killed, but the passengers must survive in the Andes until rescue arrives. In addition to the heroic pilots, the characters include a pop singer, an alcoholic comedian, an attractive liquor saleswoman (a volatile combination), a murderer on his way to trial, a black doctor, a shy school teacher, another doctor who goes insane and becomes the witch doctor of a local tribe, and the requisite stewardesses. Leonard Nimoy plays a lawyer with a few ideas about survival.

1971

ASSAULT ON THE WAYNE

Premier: January 12, 1971

Running Time: 74 minutes

PRODUCTION CREDITS; Teleplay: Jackson Gillis; Producer: Bruce Lansbury; Director: Marvin Chomsky; Director of Photography: Howard R. Schwartz; Music: Leigh Stevens; Art Director: William Campbell; Editor: Donald R. Rode; Executive Consultant: Howie Horwitz; In Charge of Project Development: Thomas L. Miller; Supervising Music Editor: Jack Hunsaker; Supervising Sound Editor: Douglas Grindstaff; Sound Mixer: Dominick Gaffey; Recorded by: Glen Glenn Sound; Unit Manager: James Nicholson; Assistant Director: Robert Birnbaum; Set Decorator: Pierre W. Ludlam; Wardrobe/Men: Jan Kemp; Wardrobe/Women: Jennifer Parsons; Special Photographic Effects: Westheimer Co.; Casting: Jim Merrick; Makeup Artist: Hal Lierley; Property Master: Ted Cook; Special Effects: Jonnie Burke; Chrysler Vehicles Furnished By Chrysler Corporation; Supervising Art Director: Bill Ross; Post Production Supervisor: Edward Milkis; Casting Supervisor: Mildred Gusse; Executive Production Manager: Ted Leonard; Production Manager: Sam Strangis; Executive Vice-President In Charge of Production: Douglas S. Cramer

CAST; **Commander Phil Kettenring: Leonard Nimoy**; Lt. Commander Dave Burston: Lloyd Haynes; Orville Kelly: Keenan Wynne; The Admiral: Joseph Cotten; Dr. Frank Reardon: William Windom; Dr. Emile Dykers: Malachi Throne; Lt. Commander Skip Langley: Dewey Martin; Clarence Karp (The Imposter): Gordon Hoban; Ensign Sandover: Sam Elliott; Ellington: Ivor Barry; Corky Schmidt: Ron Masak; Lt. Manners: Lee Stanley; Paine: Paul Sears; Lt. Benson: Dale Tarter; English Scientist: John Winston; Cab Driver: Henry Olek; Mrs. Karp: Ellen Tucker; The Real Clarence Karp: Dave Turner; Seaman: Bo Johnson; Shore Patrolman (Marine): Bill Keller; Radio Operator: Larry McCormick; Sonarman: Bobby Herbeck; Radarman: Jim Beach

A taxicab arrives in front of a small, residential home in San Diego and picks up a sailor. The cab drives off but then stops in a secluded area where the driver turns around and shoots the sailor to death.Another man assumes the sailor's identity and is dropped off at the San Diego Naval Base.

A submarine is boarding for a special mission and the imposter is one of the newly assigned crew members.

The Admiral pulls up and hands the sealed orders for the mission to Lt. Commander Kettenring (Leonard Nimoy).They discuss what is known, that the the sub is to be used as a test site for the ABM system.One of the crew members for this mission is a civilian scientist.

Karp (the imposter) makes himself at home.

Phil Kettenring reacquaints himself with an old friend, Orville Kelly, a hard drinker who's a good-natured sort but who recently enjoyed himself too much and wound up getting busted down in rank.

Commander Kettenring has Ensign Sandover inventory everything which has been brought aboard to make sure nothing potentially dangerous has been smuggled aboard the sub.

The submarine gets underway and submerges.

Kettenring talks to the doctor, whom he encounters carrying Kettenring's file.The Commander is sensitive about this because he had medical problems on his last mission.

In his cabin, Kettenring opens his top secret orders.The submarine is to head for a point near New Zealand.

Kettenring visits Dr. Dykers (Malachi Throne) to learn more about the equipment he brought aboard.It consists of two computers which will be used in the missile control system.They are in a special safe which Kettenring orders sealed with a lock attached for which only the Commander will have the key.As Kettenring walks off, we see that Dr. Dykers has found a sailor to assist him aboard the submarine.It is Karp, the imposter.

Karp reports to Dr. Reardon (William Windom), the ship's doctor, who is also part of whatever conspiracy is afoot.Just before Karp entered, the doctor had given Kettenring some "vitamin" pills.

The stress of the voyage seems to be getting to Kettenring.He seems to be on edge and keeps popping pills.

Dr. Dykers is annoyed that his personal property has been searched, including his camera, which Kettenring returns, minus the film.

Dr. Reardon gives Kettenring a shot of "B complex."

The submarine arrives at its destination.They immediately pick up an S.O.S. from the nearby island.They argue about how to proceed but Kettenring finally agrees to send a rescue party ashore.The rescue raft contains Dr. Reardon, Ensign Sandover and others.They climb up a steep cliff path and arrive at the tent containing the injured naturalist and his companions.

Aboard the sub, Orville Kelly tells Kettenring that he is suspicious of Karp.

On the island, Sandover suspects that something isn't right and he goes outside to radio back to the sub.But he has been followed by one of the men from the tent and is shot.Sandover is not heard from again.

Dr. Reardon brings the "injured" naturalist aboard the sub to more properly treat him.Kettenring is insistent about Sandover's body being found, even if he did fall from the cliff as is believed.

Kettenring collapses into his bunk and is given three more pills to take.Kettenring then falls asleep.

Dr. Reardon confers with the supposedly injured man.Just then Lt. Commander Burston (Lloyd Haynes) walks in on them, but he is part of the conspiracy as well.

Kettenring had been given a typhoid toxin which he is fighting off.The pills Reardon had given him would have killed him, but the Commander was suspicious and palmed them rather than swallow them.

The conspirators gather.They have two bombs to plant.Karp is setting the bombs to blow in 60 minutes.

Orville Kelly is still suspicious of Karp and has been following him.After he finds a cable cut in the radio room, he goes to Kettenring, who wakes up.

In the control room, sonar has picked up a vessel converging on their course.It is the pick-up ship for the conspirators.

Kettenring enters the control room and sees that they are off course.His shouting makes him appear delirious and he's overpowered and subdued.

Kelly has followed Karp and sees him planting a bomb.They fight and the commotion causes the bomb to explode.

In the confusion, Kettenring slips out to the radio room and finds that the computer controls have been stolen.Burston jumps Kettenring and they fight.A gun goes off and Burston dies.Kettenring had known the man for 15 years.

The other bomb is set to explode in 8 minutes—Burston had revealed that to Kettenring before they fought.

Dr. Reardon and the English scientist try to escape. A helicopter arrives and from another hatch Kettenring uses a rifle to shoot Reardon. The conspirators are captured and the helicopter flees.

But they still must find the second bomb. As they prepare to abandon ship, Kelly and some men find the bomb and disarm it.

All is secure. Phil, who had been unwilling to give his ex-wife a chance, now realizes how wrong he can be about people since he never really knew Dave Burston as well as he thought he had. He prepares to send his ex-wife a message.

CATLOW

Released October 21, 1971

An M-G-M Picture

103 minutes

(British title: **Maverick Gold**)

PRODUCTION CREDITS: Producer: Evan Lloyd; Director: Sam Wanamaker; 2nd Unit Director/Supervising Editor: John Glen; Action sequences staged by: Bob Simmons; Screenplay: Scot Finch & J.J. Griffith; Based on the novel by Louis L'Amour; Photography: Alan Killick; Art Direction: Herbert Smith; Sprcial Effects: Kit West; Sound: Wally Milner & Len Abbott; Wardrobe: Augustin Jimenez; Makeup: Ramon De Diego & Jose Antonio Sanchez; Hairstyles: Josefina Rubio; Production Supervisor: Ronnie Bear; Production Managers: Tadeo Villalba & Diego Siempre; Assistant Director: Jose Maria Ochoa; Filmed in Almeria, Spain, in Panavision and Metrocolor.

CAST: Catlow: Yul Brynner; Marshal Ben Cowan: Richard Crenna; **Orville Miller: Leonard Nimoy;** Rosita: Daliah Lavi; Christina: Jo Ann Pflug; Merridew: Jeff Corey; Rio: Michael Delano; Recalde: Julian Mateos; Caxton: David Ladd; Mrs. Frost: Bessie Love; Oley: Bob Logan; Keleher: John Clark; Dutch: Dan Van Heusen; Sanchez: Cass Martin; General: Jose Nieto; Captain Vargar: Angel Del Pozo; Pesqueria: Victor Israel; Sara: Erika Lopez; Pedro: Tito Garcia; Jose: Antonia Padilla; Alberto: Rafael Albaicin; Fernandez: Alejandro Encisco; Roots: Ralph Brown; Parkman: Walter Coy; Otis: Allen Russell; Cattle Boss: Per Barclay; 1st Drover: David Thomson; 2nd Drover: Jose Laurens; Tarahumara: Florencio Amarilla; Tonkawa Indian: Raul Castro

Catlow (Yul Brynner) is an outlaw who makes his living by rounding up stray cattle; Ben Cowan (Richard Crenna), an old friend, is sent to arrest him. Rescued by Catlow's gang after an assault by Indians, Cowan is helpless— but Catlow, surprisingly, surrenders to him anyway, only to escape later and head for Mexico. Catlow devises a plan to relieve the Mexican army of two million dollars worth of gold. Cowan lags behind in his pursuit but befriends a young Mexican officer who agree to help him. Along the way, he falls in love with his new friend's beautiful cousin Christina.

Cowan discovers that the gold is Confederate bullion and tries to claim it for the U.S.A., but Catlow's men steal it and head for the border. Catlow's girlfriend, jilted, rounds up a gang and gives chase. After battling Indians, Catlow and crew are captured by the Mexican army and handed over to Cowan.

Orville Miller (Nimoy), a gunman hired by the cattlemen of Texas, has been tracking Catlow, too, and chooses to open fire at this point.

Cowan is wounded; Catlow gets his gun and kills the assassin, puts on the Marshall's badge, and heads back to the U.S.A. with his men and the gold. Cowan is left behind, to be nursed by Christina, a prospect which doesn't give him any cause for complaint.

1972

REX HARRISON PRESENTS SHORT STORIES OF LOVE/ THREE FACES OF LOVE "KISS ME AGAIN, STRANGER" (TV Movie)

First aired 12/15/72 on NBC

A Universal/NBC-TV Production

PRODUCTION CREDITS: Executive Producer: William Sackheim; Producer: Herbert Hirschman; Associate Producer: Rita Dillon; Director: Arnold Laven; Unit Manager: Carter DeHaven; Teleplay: Arthur Dales; Coordinator: Tip Corbin; Casting Director: Bob Edmiston; Cameraman: Jack Marta; 1st Assistant Director: Lou Watt; 2nd Assistant Director: Bill Pool; Propmen: Vernon Ted Ross; Art Director: Bob Luthart; Set Director: Harry Gordon; Special Effects: Don Walters

CAST: **Mick: Leonard Nimoy**; Girl: Juliet Mills; Fred: Donald Moffat; Doris: Diane Webster; Man: William Beckley; Bus Conductor: Brian Gaffikin; Proprietor: Eric Christmas; R.A.F. Private: Peter Church; Usherette: Vickie Anderson; Bobby: Gerald S. Peters

Leonard plays the role of Mick in this third of the pilot for a proposed romantic anthology series. Mick is a demobilized RAF man trying to get by in London after World War Two. Someone is murdering RAF officers by stabbing them.

A shy, quiet man, Mick meets a girl who is never named (Juliet Mills); she seems interested in him, even though she blames the air force for destroying her family. They spend some time together; when he loosens a button on his jacket, she cuts it loose for him—and produces a big pair of scissors to do the job. Even though it was the Germans who bombed London, the girl makes no distinction regarding nationality; the planes dropped bombs from the sky. Mick points out that he only drove a truck, and asks if she'll be his girlfriend. She leaves him and walks home alone.

Mick thinks about the girl a great deal that night. Later, the news announces another killing, with the extra information that the culprit has been caught. Mick knows its the girl, and goes to visit her in prison. The war has left her somewhat unhinged, hence her series of murders of the people she believes responsible for the wartime bombings. She let him go because she liked him, but felt compelled to kill someone else in his place. He gives her his ring, which she earlier refused, and leaves, saddened by her fate.

This was more of a mood piece than a suspense story, focusing more on Mick's loneliness and the damage done by war than on any mad slasher plot schemes. Although there is of course the chance that the girl will kill him— it's pretty obvious that she's the killer— it is all played in a rather subdued, understated style, which makes Leonard's performance, and that of Juliet Mills, all the more effective.

1973

BAFFLED!

U.S. Television Premiere: January 30, 1973

Released theatrically in Great Britain in 1971

Prints run from 90 to 96 minutes. In Eastmancolor.

An ITC/Arena production

PRODUCTION CREDITS; Executive Producer: Normal Felton; Writer: Theodore Apstein; Director: Philip Leacock; Producer: Philip Leacock; Associate Producer: John Oldknow; Production Manager: Malcolm Christopher; Assistant Director: Michael Dryhurst; Director of Photography: Ken Hodges, B.S.C.; Editor: Bill Blunden; Art Director: Harry Pottle; Music Composed and Conducted by:

Richard Hill; Sound Editor: John Ireland; Sound Recording: John Mitchell, Gordon K. McCallum; Costume Supervisor: Elsa Fennell; Hairdresser: Eileen Warwick; Color: Eastman Colour

CAST; Tom Chester Kovack: Leonard Nimoy; Michele Brent: Susan Hampshire; Andrea Glenn: Vera Miles; Jennifer Glenn: Jewel Blanch; Mrs. Farraday: Rachel Roberts; Louise Sanford: Valerie Taylor; George Tracewell: Ray Brooks; Peggy Tracewell: Angharad Rees; Mr. Verelli: Christopher Benjamin; John Parrish/Sanford: Mike Murray; Hopkins: Ewan Roberts; Dr. Reed: Milton Johns; TV interviewer: Al Mancini; Stage Door Keeper: John Rae; Cleaning Lady: Patsy Smart; Track Announcer: Shane Rimmer; Racetrack Mechanic: Roland Brand; Doctor: Bill Hutchinson; Announcer's Assistant: Frank Mann; Ambulance Man: Michael Sloan; Policeman: Dan Meaden

Race car driver Tom Kovack (Leonard Nimoy) is leading in a race when he suddenly has a vision of a strange looking house.He swerves and almost crashes.Then he suddenly seems to be driving on a country road headed straight for a hay wagon and he spins out of the race track.As he's spinning out he sees a woman and a girl and hears the words, "It's Windom in Devon, dear."Kovack walks away from the wreck, unhurt but very confused.He's also not afraid to talk about what happened to him.

The next day, on a television talk show, Kovack discusses his apparent hallucination.Michele Brent is watching the show and is convinced that Tom really say something of significance.

Andrea Glenn, a movie star, and her daughter, Jennifer, are in a limousine on their way to the airport.They're about to leave on a trip and Andrea says, "It's Windom in Devon, dear."They are flying over to reunite with Andrea's ex-husband (who is also the girl's father) whom neither has seen in eleven years.

Michele Brent tracks down Kovack and quizzes him about his vision.She has him sketch the manor house he saw.He finds all this difficult to take seriously but he complies.She recognizes his sketch and shows him a photo of manor homes in Devon, which Kovack identifies.Michele wants Tom to help the woman in his vision, but he thinks this is all pretty far-fetched stuff.

Andrea and Jennifer arrive at Windom in Devon, but Duncan is nowhere to be seen.

Kovack is about to take a shower when he gets a phone call.It's Michele's service leaving a message as to where she can be located in England.He's planning to go to England anyway, but to chase cars, not visions.He hangs up the phone and starts walking across the room when the view from his window abruptly changes from the skyline of the city to the manor house again.He sees himself enter it and fall over a railing into the sea.He comes to his senses again lying on his run, soaking wet.

Andrea and Jennifer still haven't heard from Duncan and are becoming concerned.

Kovack arrives in England and looks up Michele.He tries to rationalize his vision except for the nagging fact that he couldn't have just stumbled into his shower since he'd been soaked with salt water.Michele makes reservations for them an Windom and they plan to arrive separately.

In London, Michele's driving makes him nervous.He leaves to arrive at Devon first.

Andrea and Jennifer visit the home of Duncan Sanford's cousin, a kindly old woman in a wheelchair.She expresses surprise over Duncan's absence.

Kovack arrives at Windom and recognizes it for certain.Mrs. Farraday, the owner, introduces him to Andrea and Jennifer.He recognizes who Andrea is then.

Michele Brent arrives and Kovack meets her.

That night, Jennifer secretly meets her father in the summer house.He swears her to secrecy and gives her a pendant to wear which only she can touch.

The next day Jennifer appears to be three years older, as though she has aged from 12 to 15 overnight.

Tom has a vision of a hand squeezing something from a broad leaf into a red glass.He finds Andrea about to drink from a red glass and he manages to break it.

Andrea announces that she and Jennifer are planning to leave the following day.

Tom and Michele see Jennifer with Mrs. Farrady who now looks much younger.

Mrs. Farrady gives Andrea another red glass and the woman becomes very ill.

In the greenhouse out back, Tom and Michele find the plant which he say.It's poisonous.

They learn about an address for Duncan's old friend, John Parrish, and Michele goes there in hopes of tracing him.

Mrs. Farraday secretly meets the same man that Jennifer did.

Kovack follows Jennifer that night and is lured towards a place on the pathway along the cliff where the wooden railing has been weakened. Tom falls through and into the water, barely missing the rocks.

Michele finds the shop once owned by John Parrish. It was destroyed in a fire a few months before and it owner supposedly died in the blaze.

Kovack goes driving with Michele and they're followed by a black van. They investigate the van and Michele is kidnapped. Tom gives chase. It's a long chase. He finally forces the van off the road and finds the unconscious Michele inside. She never say who struck her.

Jennifer has perceived that Tom and Michele did not just meet at Windom and tells her mother, who mentions it to Mrs. Farrady. When Kovack sees Mr. Verelli jogging back to the manor house, he assumes that this was the driver who fled the van and begins to threaten him. Mrs. Farrady uses that as a perfect excuse to tell Tom and Michele to pack up and get out the following morning.

That night Tom and Michele discuss what they know. He jots down notes but when he looks he finds that he has written, "Duncan Sanford Is Dead."

Andrea hears her daughter calling to her that night and runs out to the summer house where she sees the girl lying on the floor, apparently dead. She faints. When she awakens back in the manor house, she's told that she was found outside and Jennifer is standing there, in good health. Andrea is very upset and wants to leave.

The following morning Tom and Michele are packing to leave and stalling as much as they can.

Tom sees someone enter a secret panel and he follows them. In the basement he surprises Verelli in the wine cellar. He'd had a vision of Verelli with a blood meat cleaver but now his vision sharpens and he sees that the man is just a harmless wholesale butcher.

Michele finds out that Louise Sanford has lived in her nearby cottage for only two weeks. She also secures evidence that Duncan Sanford died eight months before.

While investigating the basement, Tom and Michele are locked in the bottom of the elevator shaft.

Jennifer confesses to her mother that she's been seeing Duncan. They go upstairs to see Louise, who tells Andrea that Duncan is dead. Then Andrea finds that she is locked in the tower room with Louise, who rises from her wheelchair. Louise knows about Jennifer's powers and intends to use them. She tries to force Andrea to sign a letter.

Michele tells Tom to try to use his powers to open the door. Suddenly the door opens, and it's Verelli who came back for another bottle of wine and heard them behind the door. They come upstairs and see Jennifer wearing the mystic pendant. When Mrs. Farrady sees them she flees in her car.

Tom approaches Jennifer with his arms crossed in front of him to try to remove the necklace. But Jennifer removes it herself and then tries to run up the stairs. She falls and breaks the pendant.

Mrs. Farrady suddenly ages again and becomes hysterical, crashing her car, and is killed.

In the tower room, Louise tries to kill Andrea, but Tom breaks in and he and the "old woman" get into a knock-down, drag-out fight. Soon "Louise" is unmasked as being John Parrish in disguise. They battle and Parrish tries to push Tom off the balcony with a wheelchair, but instead the momentum carries him over to the rocks below.

They all leave the next morning. Jennifer is back to normal and Andrea is fine. Tom tells Michele that he'll miss her and then has a sudden vision of a blind man in Paris who looks like Parrish. He asks Michele to accompany him and she agrees. And they're off on another jaunt with danger!

This was originally made in England in 1971 and played there theatrically, although it wasn't seen in the U.S. until 1973. ITC wanted this to serve as a pilot for a new series, but Leonard was just fresh from five continuous years on series television (three on *Star Trek* immediately followed by two on *Mission: Impossible*) and he had no interest in returning to that daily grind. This was at the time when a number of series were being produced in England featuring American stars, such as Tony Curtis, Robert Vaughn, Gene Barry, Barbara Bain and Martin Landau and clearly aimed at the lucrative American syndication market.

A sly joke which many people probably didn't catch occurs when Michele asks Tom why he didn't recognize this famous American movie star when he saw her screaming in his vision. He replies that he'd never seen a movie in which she'd screamed. Vera Miles (the actress he refers to) is most widely known for her supporting role in *Psycho in* which she does a lot of screaming.

Although it could be argued that this was first done in *From Russia With Love,* it was *Mission: Impossible which* established as an "acceptable" plot device (because they did it so often) the science fiction concept that a person wearing a mask could successfully impersonate someone and escape even at close scrutiny.In the middle of Tom's fight with "Louise Sanford," the old lady is revealed to be John Parrish wearing a mask.As is typical for such scenes, it's the old woman we see at first, but as the mask is dislodged in the fight, suddenly it becomes an obvious mask rather than the incredibly "life-like" appurtenance it was a moment before, and instead of the old woman it is the young male actor who is tearing away the mask. When this was done in the James Bond film it was no more than a one-time throw-away bit.*Mission: Impossible turned* it into a crutch to shore up plots and it's been used that way ever since.The fact that no such masks exist doesn't seem to bother film-makers who know that even elaborate make-up looks like just what it is if you get very close to a person.On screen a person in make-up must be perfectly lit so that it doesn't look phony.

Two versions of this film exist.On American TV it was just called *Baffled,* but in England (and apparently on video) an exclamation point was added so that it becomes *Baffled!* The British version also has much smaller lettering for the credits just like all theatrical films do and are barely legible on the television screen.

The music is typical British TV show music, sounding like a bad imitation of Laurie Johnson's *Avengers music.*

The cinematography is very good, though, particularly on the exterior shots.One weird bit used throughout the film is the strange slow-motion closeup of people hanging upside down as they're falling.This is an approach I can't recall ever having seen used quite this way at any time either before or since this film.It's very effective.Other effective scenes include Kovack in his hotel room when he turns to see the manor hour through his highrise window.It's quite dramatic and looks to have been accomplished on a soundstage by substituting the projected skyline shot with the manor house at night.It creates an eerie and unnerving effect and it's much sharper than it would have been had it been accomplished by an optical effect.

As the good natured Tom Kovack, Leonard really seems to be enjoying himself in the role.Filmed in 1971, the actor was still in possession of his dashing youthful qualities which served him in good stead when playing the leading man in action roles.

As Michele Brent, Susan Hampshire plays her role with an unrelieved single-mindedness.She's obsessive about the occult and always certain that she's right.I found this somewhat discomforting as she reminds me of many people who are interested in the occult in reality but who have nothing more substantial than their own hopes to pin their beliefs on.Other than Michele Brent's interest and knowledge of the occult, we learn nothing about her.Characters in this story tend toward the one-dimensional in order to advance the plot.The movie star is just a movie star.Her daughter is just her daughter.Tom Kovack is a race car driver.Michele is an occult researcher.But we never find out who they are as people.These deficiencies really don't show up in the story when you're viewing it, but only afterwards when you start thinking about it.

The British version is slightly longer (by a couple of minutes) from what was originally aired on TV in 1973.The extra time seems to be largely in the car chase between Tom and the black van, with some time possibly added in the fight in the tower room.

1973

THE ALPHA CAPER

TV Movie: First aired 10/6/73, ABC-TV

PRODUCTION CREDITS: Executive Producer: Harve Bennett; Associate Producer: Arnold Tucker; Producer: Aubrey Schenck; Director: Robert Michael Lewis; Photography: Enzo A. Martinelli; Music: Oliver Nelson; Teleplay: Elroy Schwartz and Steven Bochco; Art Direction: John J. Lloyd; Editor: Richard Belding

CAST: Mark Forbes: Henry Fonda; **Mitch: Leonard Nimoy;** Scat: James McEachin; Tudor: Larry Hagman; Lee Saunders: John Marley; Hilda: Elena Verdugo; Harry Balsam: Noah Berry; Harlan Moss: Tom Troupe; Minister: Woodrow Parfey; Policeman: Vic Tayback; Police Captain: Kenneth Tobey; John Woodbury: Paul Kent; Henry Kellner: James B. Sikking; Tow Truck Driver: Paul Sorensen; Sergeant: Wally Taylor

Mark Forbes (Henry Fonda) is a parole officer being forced to retire. One of his parolees dies but not before telling him about a big heist three other parolees are planning. He gets in on it; luckily, he's also involved in security for the gold shipment. Leonard Nimoy is Mitch, the electronic wizard of the team. The heist goes off perfectly, but, as in *The Lavender Hill Mob* and other pictures, fate plays tricks on the happy crooks and the tide turns. The three criminals try to convince the authorities that they had forced Mark to help them, but they all wind up in jail.

1975

THE MISSING ARE DEADLY

TV Movie: Aired 1/8/75

Lawrence Gordon Productions/20th Century Fox

PRODUCTION CREDITS: Executive Producer: Lawrence Gordon; Producer: Allen S. Epstein; Director: Don McDougall; Teleplay: Kathryn and Michael Michaelian; Photography: Tim Southcott; Music: Gil Melle; Art Director: Rodger Maus; Editor: Frank Capacchione

CAST: Dr. Ted Margolin: Ed Nelson; **Dr. Max Durov: Leonard Nimoy**; David Margolin: George O'Hanlon, Jr.; Jeff Margolin: Gary Morgan; Mr. Warren: Jose Ferrer; Michelle: Kathleen Quinlan; Mrs. Robertson: Marjorie Lord; Dr. Martinez: Armand Alzamora; Captain Franklin: John Milford; Mrs. Bates: Irene Tedrow; Grocer: Stuart Nisbet

Leonard plays Dr. Max Durov, a doctor doing research on the highly toxic Mombasa fever. Durov's boss, Dr. Ted Margolin (Ed Nelson), has two sons, one of whom, Jeff, is a bit on the disturbed side. Jeff sneaks into Durov's lab and liberates an infected mouse right before his older brother takes him camping in the mountains. Thus, the boys (and the older brother's girlfriend) have been exposed to the fever and have gone off where no one can find them! Leonard's role is essentially secondary to the search for the mouse and the boys, but he does come up with a cure for the fever in time to save the boys. Not a very inspiring film. Flat wooden and pointless, one can't help but wonder why anyone as intelligent as Leonard would have been involved in this turkey.

1978

INVASION OF THE BODY SNATCHERS

Released 12/22/78

A Philip Kaufman Film

PRODUCTION CREDITS: Producer: Robert H. Solo; Director: Philip Kaufman; Screenplay: W.D. Richter; Based on the novel "The Body Snatchers" by Jack Finney; Director of Photography: Michael Chapman; Production Designer: Charles Rosen; Editor: Douglas Stewart; Music: Denny Zeitlin; Production Manager: Alan Levine; 1st Assistant Director: Jim Bloom; 2nd Assistant Director: Toby Lavallo; Script Supervisor: Alice Tompkins; Production Assistant: Patrick Burns; Production Secretary: Joan Wellman; Makeup Effects: Thomas Burman and Edouard Henriques; Special Effects by Dell Rheaume and Russ Hessey; Camera Operator: Joe Marquette; 1st Camera Assistant: Dusty Blauvelt; 2nd Camera Assistant: Allan Blauvelt; Still Photographer: Wynn Hammer; Special Sound Effects: Ben Burtt; Sound: Art Rochester; Boom Operator: Stephen Powell; Re-Recording Mixers: Mark Berger and Andrew Wiskes; Supervising Sound Editor: Bonnie Koehler

CAST: Matthew Bennell: Donald Sutherland; Elizabeth Driscoll: Brooke Adams; **Dr. David Kibner: Leonard Nimoy**; Nancy Bellicec: Veronica Cartwright; Jack Bellicec: Jeff Goldblun; Geoffrey: Art Hindle; Katherine: Lrlia Goldoni; Running Man: Kevin McCarthy; Taxi Driver: Don Siegel; Ted Hendley: Tom Luddy; Stan: Stan Ritchie; Mr. Gianni: David Fisher; Detective: Tom Dahlgren; Boccardo: Gary Goodrow; Restaurant Owner: Jerry Walter; Chef: Maurice Argent; Street Barker: Sam Conti; Mr. Tong: Wood Moy; Mrs. Tong: R. Wong; Outraged Woman: Rose Kaufman; Beggar: Joe Bellan; Policeman #1: Sam Hiona; Policeman #2: Lee McVeigh; Rodent Man: Albert Nalbandian; School Teacher: Lee Mines

This remake of the 1950s classic stars Donald Sutherland as Matthew Bennell and Brooke Adams as Elizabeth. Kevin McCarthy, star of the original film, has a cameo which leads one to believe that he's been trying to warn humanity about the pods ever since 1956. When Elizabeth tells her friend Matthew about her boyfriend's strange behavior, he suggests that she talks to the eminent pop psychiatrist, Dr. David Kibner (Leonard Nimoy). Matthew begins to encounter more people claiming that their friends and family have changed. Kibner says that this has been happening all over, but maintains his professional demeanor at all times. He acts as an ally of the various characters as they become more and more convinced that something is seriously wrong— but he is really trying to get them to become pod people too!

Like the original, this is a creepy, suspenseful film, and Nimoy gives a good performance as the deceptive shrink, who keeps the heroes off guard by constantly trying to find some "reasonable" explanation for the strange events afflicting their city.

1979

STAR TREK: THE MOTION PICTURE

PRODUCTION CREDITS: Directed by Robert Wise; Produced by Gene Roddenberry; Screenplay by Harold Livingston; Story by alan

Dean Foster; Based on "Star Trek" created by Gene Roddenberry; Director of photography: Richard H. Kline, A.S.C.; Music by Jerry Goldsmith; Special Photographic Effects Directed by Douglas Trumbull; Special Photographic Effects Supervised by Johnn-Dykstra; Special Photographic Effects Produced by Richard Yuricich

CAST: Captain Kirk: William Shatner; **Spock: Leonard Nimoy;** Dr. McCoy: DeForest Kelley; Scotty: James Doohan; Sulu: George Takei; Dr. Chapel: Majel Barrett; Chekov: Walter Koenig; Uhura: Nichelle Nichols; Ilia: Persis Khambata; Decker: Stephen Collins; Janice Rand: Grace Lee Whitney; Klingon Captain: Mark Lenard; Alien Boy: Billy Van Zandt; Epsilon Technician: Roger Aaron Brown; Airlock Technician: Gary Faga; Commander Branch: David Gautreaux; Assistant to Rand: John D. Gowans; Cargo Deck Engineer: Howard Itzkowitz; Lt. Commander Sonak: Jon Rashad Kamal; Chief DiFalco: Marcy Lafferty; Lieutenant: Michele Ameen Billy; Chief Ross: Terence O'Connor; Lt. Cleary: Michael Rougas; Woman: Susan J. Sullivan; Crew Members: Ralph Brannen, Ralph Byers, Paula Crist, Iva Lane, Franklyn Seales, Momo Yashima; Klingon Crew Members: Jimmie Booth, Joel Kramer, Bill McTosh, Dave Moordigian, Tom Morga, Tony Rocco, Joel Shultz, Craig Thomas; Vulcan Masters: Edna Glover, Norman Stuart, Paul Weber; Yeoman: Leslie C. Howard; Technical Assistants: Sayra Hummel, Junero Jennings; Stunts: Robert Bralver, William Couch, Keith L. Jensen, John Hugh McKnight

The long-awaited feature film proves to be a bit of a fizzle, as the characters have little to do beyond looking suitably impressed by the special effects.

1980

SEIZURE: THE STORY OF KATHY MORRIS

TV-movie, first aired 1/9/80, CBS-TV

PRODUCTION CREDITS: Produced by Lee Miller ; Directed by Gerald I. Isenberg; Technical advisors: Don Kaiserman, M.D., M. Ray Rogers, M.D. and ; Connie Izay, M.D.

CAST: Kathy Morris: Penelope Milford; Dr. Richard Connought: Leonard Nimoy; Patrick Morris: Christopher Allport; Larry: Fredric Lehne; Dr. Beale: Gay Rowan; Dr. Clark: Steven Peterman; Dr. Ames: Nicholas Guest; Mr. Wilcox: Jonathan Estrin; Nina Ryan: Rita Taggart; Nurse: Shirley Batt; Bus Driver: Tom Mardirosian; Music Teacher: Lenke Peterson; Debbie: Sarah Truslow; Waitress:

Joie Magidow; Patient: Kathryn Jackson; Orderly: Arthur Trevino; Intern: Frederick Herrick

This was based on a true story. Kathy Morris (Penelope Milford) is a young woman with a promising musical career— until her frequent headaches and dizzy spells turn out to be the results of a small benign brain tumor. A seizure places her in the hospital, where neurosurgeon Dr. Richard Connought decides to remove the tumor.

The operation seems to be a fairly routine one, but the self-assured surgeon is suddenly faced with unforeseen complications. The patients brain swells and makes it impossible to excise the tumor; Dr. Connought must cut away some of the swollen tissue in order to close up Kathy's skull. The operation is unsuccessful and Kathy's life seems near its end.

Dr. Connought is rattled by this failure, and his personal life begins to unravel. His wife leaves him, and he begins to seriously doubt his surgical skills.

Kathy lives despite predictions to the contrary, but her life is still threatened. Connought operates twice more: once to remove the pressure from the swelling of her brain, and again to finally remove the tumor. Connought's faith in himself is renewed by Kathy's recovery, as the young woman's will to live and remarkable rehabilitation is depicted in the rest of the movie.

1982

A WOMAN CALLED GOLDA

TV-movie, aired 4/17 & 4/24/82

Running time: Four hours

PRODUCTION CREDITS: Executive Producer: Harve Bennett; Associate Producer: Marilyn Hall; Producer: Gene Corman; Director: Alan Gibson; Script: Harold Gast and Steven Gethers; Music: Michel Legrand; Publicist: Rupert Allan

CAST: Golda Meir: Ingrid Bergman; Young Golda: Judy Davis; Morris Meyerson: Leonard Nimoy; Ariel: Jack Thompson; King Abdullah: Nigel Hawthorne; Wingate: Barry Foster; Moshe Dayan: Yossi Graber; David Ben-Gurion: David de Keyser; Macey: Bruce Boa; Lou Kaddar: Anne Jackson; Anwar Sadat: Robert Loggia; Senator Durward: Ned Beatty; Hubert Humphrey: Franklin Cover

The true story of Golda Meir, portrayed in her youth by Judy Davis and in later life by Ingrid Bergman. Leonard Nimoy plays her husband, Morris Myerson, who ages decades over the course of this four-hour film.

The young Golda is first seen at a concert in Milwaukee with the somewhat older Morris Myerson. She is not knowledgeable about music, so he undertakes to educate her in the arts. They fall in love and want to marry, but Golda has decided to go to Palestine to live on a kibbutz. Meyerson says he will not marry her if she goes, but the next scene shows them in Palestine, on their way to the kibbutz. Morris just can't say no to Golda.

Golda adapts to the rigors of life on the kibbutz, while her husband gamely strives to fit in, even though he'd rather go back to the United States. An Arab attack on the kibbutz turns out to really be just a drill by the Haganah, the unofficial and illegal Jewish army.

Morris becomes very ill, but even this does not undermine his sardonic sense of humor. At last it is discovered that he has a mild form of malaria. He decides to leave the kibbutz; if Golda will come with him he will stay in Palestine, but otherwise he will go back to the United States. She agrees to go with him. When they leave, he gives his phonograph player to the kibbutz as a gift, as it was their only source of music.

Two years later, they are living in Jerusalem with their two young children. Golda runs into trouble at an Arab market but is rescued by an old friend from the kibbutz, who offers her a job in Tel Aviv. Morris is dismayed at this news, as he wants to stay where he is, but Golda wants the job very badly, and will not listen to his arguments.

The scene shifts to the years of World War Two. Golda is now involved in Zionist politics and is trying to obtain British training for an official Israeli army before the British withdraw. Her marriage with Morris has long before been dissolved.

In 1944, an international resolution divides Palestine between the Arabs and the Jews, setting the groundwork for what would become the modern state of Israel. At the celebrations in Jerusalem, Golda sees Morris for the first time in years. They talk about their children. Golda's political involvement often keeps her from them. Morris is proud of what Golda has accomplished. Their meeting is touching but awkward, and then Morris vanishes into the celebrating crowds.

The history of Israel proceeds, with Golda deeply involved. In 1948, the state of Israel is proclaimed. Golda becomes Minister of Labor, a post she holds for seven years.

In 1951, Morris dies. Golda's career continues for many years, including two terms as Prime Minister of Israel. She dies at the age of eighty in 1978, after living to see Anwar Sadat of Egypt make peace with Israel.

Ingrid Bergman was awarded the Brotherhood Media Award of the National Conference of Christians and Jews for her role in this film; Leonard Nimoy accepted the award on her behalf.

MARCO POLO

5/16/82, 5/17/82, 5/18/82, 5/19/82

Running time: 10 hours

CAST: Marco Polo: Ken Marshall; Niccolo Polo: Denholm Eliott; Matteo Polo: Tony Vogel; Aunt Flora: Sada Thompson; Uncle Zane: Riccardo Cucciolla; Caterina: Georgia Slowe; Marco's Mother: Anne Bancroft; Marco as a child: Alexandre Picolo; Pope Gregory X: Burt Lancaster; Patriarch: John Houseman; Doge: John Gielgud; Ali Ben Youssef: Ian McShane; Jacopo: F. Murray Abraham; Giovanni: Mario Adorf; Rustichello: David Warner; Kublai Khan: Ying Ruocheng; Empress Chabi: Beulah Khow; Prince Chinkin: Juichi Ishida; Pags-Pa: James Hong; Monica: Kathrin Dowling; Bektor: En He Sen; Nayan: Zhao Er-Kong; **Achmet Benaketi: Leonard Nimoy;** Fra' Damiano: Patrick Mower

The historical adventures of the Venetian traveller Marco Polo, who travelled to China with his merchant family and wrote his memoirs in prison after he returned, years later, as no one believed his outlandish adventures.

Leonard Nimoy plays the Turk Achmet, the regent who administers the government of China while Kublai Khan is away from the capital. A somewhat sinister character, he is not fully exploited in this drama, as Achmet was a man who used his power to get whatever he wanted, including any woman he desired. After twenty two years, the people of his province rose up against him and killed him. When Kublai Khan learned of Achmet's abuses he took the Moslem's ill-gained riches as a part of his own treasury, and had Achmet's body dug up and thrown to the dogs in the street. Unfortunately for Nimoy fans, much of this character's potential was left out of this mini-series, and he only occupied a supporting role as one of Kublai Khan's administrators.

STAR TREK II: THE WRATH OF KHAN

PRODUCTION CREDITS: Directed by Nicholas Meyer; Produced by Robert Sallin; Screenplay by Jack B. Sowards; Story by Harve Bennett and Jack B. Sowards; Based on "Star Trek" created by Gene Roddenberry; Executive Producer: Harve Bennett; Director of Photography: Gayne Rescner, A.S.C.; Production Designer: Joseph R. Jennings; Edited by William P. Dornisch; Music composed by James Horner

SPECIAL VISUAL EFFECTS PRODUCED AT INDUSTRIAL LIGHT & MAGIC

(A DIVISION OF LUCASFILM, LTD.)

CAST; Captain Kirk: William Shatner; **Spock: Leonard Nimoy;** Dr. McCoy: DeForest Kelley; Scotty: James Doohan; Sulu: George Takei; Chekov: Walter Koenig; Uhura: Nichelle Nichols; Carol: Bibi Besch; David: Merritt Butrick; Terrell: Paul Winfield; Saavik: Kirstie Alley; Khan: Ricardo Montalban; Preston: Ike Eisenmann; Jedda: John Vargas; Kyle: John Winston; Beach: Paul Kent; Cadet: Nicholas Guest; Madison: Russell Takaki; March: Kevin Sullivan; Crew Chief: Joel Marstan

The second Star Trek film picks up the slack for the action lacking in the first one, replete with Ricardo Montalban as a suitably Miltonic villain, thrilling space battles and a tragic death for Spock. Millions raged but they killed him anyway.

1984

STAR TREK III: THE SEARCH FOR SPOCK

PRODUCTION CREDITS

Directed by Leonard Nimoy; Written and Produced by Harve Bennett; Based on "Star Trek" created by Gene Roddenberry; Executive Producer: Gary Nardino; Director of Photography: Charles Correll, A.S.C.

SPECIAL VISUAL EFFECTS PRODUCED AT INDUSTRIAL LIGHT & MAGIC

CAST; Captain Kirk: William Shatner; **Spock: Leonard Nimoy;** Dr. McCoy: DeForest Kelley; Scotty: James Doohan; Sulu: George Takei; Chekov: Walter Koenig; Uhura: Nichelle Nichols; Saavik: Robin Curtis; David: Merritt Butrick; Trainee Foster: Phil Morris; "Mr. Adventure": Scott McGinnis; Commander Morrow: Robert Hooks; Spock, aged 9: Carl Steven; Spock, age 13: Vadia Potenza; Spock, age 17: Stephen Manley; Spock, age 25: Joe W. Davis; MERCHANTSHIP: Captain: Paul Sorenson; Valkris: Cathie Shirriff; KLINGONS: Kruge: Christopher Lloyd; Torg: Stephen Liska; Maltz: John Larroquette; Sergeant: Dave Cadiente; Gunner #1: Bob Cummings; Gunner #2: Branscombe Richmond; USS GRISSOM: Captain Estaban: Philip Richard Allen; Helm: Jeanne Mori; Communications: Mario Marcelino; THE BAR: Alien: Allan Miller; Waitress: Sharon Thomas; Civilian Agent: Conroy Gedeon; THE EXCELSIOR: Captain Styles: James B. Sikking; First Officer: Miguel Ferrer; THE VULCANS: Sarek: Mark Lenard; Child: Katherine Blum; High Priestess: Dame Judith Anderson; OTHERS: Prison Guard #1: Gary Faga; Prison Guard #2: Douglas Allan Shanklin; Woman In Cafeteria: Grace Lee Whitney; STAND-INS: Robin Kellick, Phil Weyland, Kimberly L. Ryusaki, Steve Blalock; VOICES: Spock screams: Frank Welker; Enterprise Computer: Teresa E. Victor; Flight Recorder: Harve Bennett; Space Dock Controller: Judi Durand; Elevator Voice: Frank Force; Background Voices: The Loop Group

Proving that you can have your tragedy and eat it too, Spock comes back, but at least they had more tact than, say, Spielberg, and waited until the next movie to pull the resurrection stunt. It's well done, too, and enables Nimoy to stay behind the camera for the bulk of the film.

THE SUN ALSO RISES

(NBC) 12/9/84 & 12/10/84

Running time: 4 hours

PRODUCTION CREDITS: Exec. Producer: John Furia, Jr.; Co-Producer: Robert L. Joseph; Director: James Goldstone; Teleplay: Robert L. Joseph; Based on the novel by Ernest Hemingway; Assoc. Producer: Jean Pierre Avice; Film Editors: Richard E. Rabjohn, Robert P. Seppey; Production Designer: Francois de Lamothe; Art Directors: Jacques Brizzio, Jose Maria Tapiador; Director of Photography: Jacques Robin; Music: Billy Goldenberg; Costume Designer: Catherine Gorne; Make-up: Antoine Garabedian; Production Consultant: Jay Weston

CAST; Lady Brett Ashley: Jane Seymour; Jake Barnes: Hart Bochner; Robert Cohn: Robert Carradine; Bill Gorton: Zeljko Ivanek; Georgette: Stephane Audran; Nicole: Elisabeth Borgine; Pedro Romero: Andrea Occhipinti; Special Guest Star: Ian Carleson as Mike; **Special Guest Appearance by Leonard Nimoy as the Count**

Although actually appearing in the novel in a small role, here The Count is expanded to inject an ominous undertone to the proceedings, and his presence allows the story to build to a startling climax.

1986

STAR TREK IV: THE VOYAGE HOME

PRODUCTION CREDITS: Directed by Leonard Nimoy; Produced by Harve Bennett; Story by Leonard Nimoy and Harve Bennett;

Screenplay by Steve Meerson & Peter Krikes, ; Harve Bennett & Nicholas Meyer; Based upon "Star Trek" created by Gene Roddenberry; Executive Producer: Ralph Winter; Director of Photography: Donald Peterman, A.S.C.; Music by Leonard Rosenman; VISUAL EFFECTS PRODUCED AT INDUSTRIAL LIGHT & MAGIC

CAST; Captain Kirk: William Shatner; **Spock: Leonard Nimoy;** Dr. McCoy: DeForest Kelley; Scotty: James Doohan; Sulu: George Takei; Chekov: Walter Koenig; Uhura: Nichelle Nichols; Amanda: Jane Wyatt; Gillian: Catherine Hicks; Sarek: Mark Lenard; Lt. Saavik: Robin Curtis; Federation Council President: Robert Ellenstein; Klingon Ambassador: John Schuck; Admiral Cartwright: Brock Peters; Starfleet Communications Officer: Michael Snyder; Starfleet Display Officer: Michael Berryman; Saratoga Science Officer: Mike Brislane; Commander Rand: Grace Lee Whitney; Alien Communications Officer: Jane Wiedlin; Starship Captain: Vijay Amritraj; Commander Chapel: Majel Barrett; Saratoga Helmsman: Nick Ramus; Controller #1: Thaddeus Golas; Controller #2: Martin Pistone; IN OLD SAN FRANCISCO: Bob Briggs: Scott DeVenney; Lady In Tour: Viola Stimpson; 1st Garbageman: Phil Rubinstein; 2nd Garbageman: John Miranda; Antique Store Owner: Joe Knowland; Waiter: Bob Sarlatte; Cafe Owner: Everett Lee; Joe: Richard Harder; Nichols: Alex Henteloff; Pilot: Tony Edwards; Elderly Patient: Eve Smith; Intern #1: Tom Mustin; Intern #2: Greg Karas; Young Doctor: Raymond Singer; Doctor #1: David Ellenstein; Doctor #2: Judy Levitt; Usher: Teresa E. Victor; Jogger: James Menges; Punk On Bus: Kirk Thatcher; FBI Agent: Jeff Lester; Shore Patrolman: Joe Lando; CDO: Newell Tarrant; Electronic Technicians: Mike Timoney, Jeffrey Martin; Marine Sergeant: 1st Sgt. Joseph Naradzay, USMC; Marine Lieutenant: 1st Lt. Donald W. Zautke, USMC

Nimoy directs the most enjoyable Star Trek feature, and the entire cast obviously enjoyed themselves; Spock goes to the 20th Century but never resorts to the use of a stocking cap.

1987

THREE MEN AND A BABY

PRODUCTION CREDITS: Directed by Leonard Nimoy; Produced by Ted Field and Robert W. Cort; Screenplay by James Orr and Jim Cruickshank; Based on "Trois Hommes et un Couffin" by Coline Serreau; Executive Producer: Jean Francois Lepetit; Co-produced by Edward Teets; Director of Photography: Adam Greenberg; Production Designer: Peter Larkin; Edited by Michael A. Stevenson, A.C.E.; Music by Marvin Hamlisch; Casting by Diane Crittenden

CAST; Peter: Tom Selleck; Michael: Steve Guttenberg; Jack: Ted Danson; Sylvia: Nancy Travis; Rebecca: Margaret Colin; Patty: Alexandra Amini; Woman at Gift Shop: Francine Beers; Mary: Lisa Blair/Michelle Blair; Detective Melkowitz: Philip Bosco; Dramatic Actress: Barbara Budd; Handsome Man at Party: Michael Burgess; Angelyne: Claire Cellucci; Man at Party #1: Eugene Clark; Jan Clopatz: Derek de Lint; Tawnya: Michele Duquet; Telephone Installer: David Ferry; Grocery Store Clerk: David Foley; Vince: Paul Guilfoyle; Mrs. Hathaway: Cynthia Harris; Satch: Earl Hindman; Jack's Mother: Celeste Holme; Cab Driver: Mario Joyner; Detective #1: Gary Klar; One of Jack's Girls: Christine Kossak; Detective #2: Joe Lynn; Security Guard: Edward D. Murphy; Gate Attendant: Jacqueline Murphy; Gift Shop Clerk: Colin Quinn; Mounted Policeman: Thomas Quinn; Edna: Jackie Richardson; Paul Milner: John Gould Rubin; Cherise: Camilla Scott; Swimming Instructor: Danielle Scott; Vanessa: Sharolyn Sparrow; Sally: Louise Vallance; Adam: Jonathan Whitaker

Three carefree bachelors find a baby on their doorstep. They're all ladies' men so the figure that one of them must have fathered the child, but they don't know who as there's no note. . .so all three take the baby in, and learn how to act responsibly after years of not taking life seriously. A huge hit, both this version and the original French film on which it is based.

1988

THE GOOD MOTHER

Released November, 1988

PRODUCTION CREDITS: Directed by Leonard Nimoy; Screenplay by Michael Bortman; Based upon the novel by Sue Miller; Produced by Arnold Glimcher; Director of Photography: David Watkin; Production Designer: Stan Jolley; Film Editor: Peter Berger, A.S.C.; Costume Designer: Susan Becker; Casting by Barbara Shapiro

CAST; Anna: Diane Keaton; Leo: Liam Neeson; Muth: Jason Robards; Grandfather: Ralph Bellamy; Grandmother: Teresa Wright; Brian: James Naughton; Molly: Asia Viera; Frank Williams: Joe Morton; Ursula: Katey Sagal; Aunt Rain: Margaret Bard; Anna's Mother: Nancy Beatty; Anna's Father: Barry Belchamber; Young Anna: Mairon Bennett; Young Bobby: Zachary Bennett; Eric: Scott Brunt; Arch: Eugene A. Clark; Court Clerk: Elizabeth Clarke; Celia: Beverly Cooper; Uncle Rain: Philip Eckman; Garrett: Greg Ellwand; Neighborhood Woman #1: Sheila Ferrini; Alex: Adam Furfaro; Neighborhood Woman #2: Donna Galligan; Judge: David Gardner; Neighbor Kid #1: Teal Gennaro; Bobby's Wife: Gloria

Gifford; Nanny: Diane Gordon; Muth's Secretary: Joyce Gordon; Babe: Tracy Griffith; Ticket Agent: Tammy Heaberlin; Longshoreman's Son: Daniel J. Howard; Emcee: Silar Jr.; Eddie: Howard Jerome; Bobby *(older): Marvin Karon; Jonathon: Robert Keppy; Uncle Orrie: Charles Kimbrough; Catherine's Husband: Tim Lee; Catherine: Nina Linder; Neighbor Kid #2: Richard LeBranti; Neighbor Kid #2: Brian Mason; Dr. Payne: Fred Melamed; Mrs. Harkessian: Monique Mojica; Longshoreman: Paul MacCallum; Butch McClendon: Butch McClendon; Aunt Weezie: Maureen McRae; Orrie's Wife: Patricia Phillips; William: Karl Pruner; Babe's '64 Boyfriend: Branko Racki; Bartender: Gary Reidt; Uncle Weezie: Terrence Slater; Court Clerk: Heather Smith; Jocelyn: Tina Teggart; Babe's Boyfriend: Rod Wilson; Court Bailiff: Cliff Woolner; Mark: Brian Young; Stunt Coordinator: Branko Racki

A well-acted dramatic film, based on Sue Miller's best selling 1986 novel. Anna (Diane Keaton) is the divorced mother of six-year old Molly. Anna is shy and insecure but blossoms when she becomes involved with Leo, an Irish sculptor (Liam Neeson). But the open-minded sexual attitudes which develop in Anna's home leads her priggish ex-husband (James Naughton) to mount a custody dispute, which hinges on the possibility that Leo may have molested Molly (basically, she saw him nude, and that was about it). The bulk of the story is a compelling courtroom drama examining sexual mores and other aspects of contemporary society.

1989

STAR TREK V: THE FINAL FRONTIER

PRODUCTION CREDITS: Director: William Shatner; Producer: Harve Bennett; Exec. Producer: Ralph Winter; Screenplay by David Loughery; Based on a story by William Shatner, Harve Bennett and David Loughery; Music composed by Jerry Goldsmith; Director of Photography: Andrew Laszlo; Art Direction and Costume Design: Nilo Rodis-Jamero; Editor: Peter Berger; Production Designer: Herman Zimmerman; Set Design: Ronald R. Wilkinson, Richard Frank McKenzie, Andrew Neskoromny, Antoinette Gordon; Sound: David Ronne; Special Visual Effects Supervisor: Dick Rauh; Yosemite Climbing Sequence Director: Robert Carmichael

CAST; Captain Kirk: William Shatner; **Spock: Leonard Nimoy;** Dr. McCoy: DeForest Kelley; Scotty: James Doohan; Sulu: George Takei; Chekov: Walter Koenig; Uhura: Nichelle Nichols; Sybok: Laurence Luckinbill; St. John Talbot: David Warner; Korrd: Charles Cooper; Caithlin Dar: Cynthia Gouw; Captain Klaa: Todd

Bryant; Vixis: Spice Williams; J'onn: Rex Holman; "God": George Murdock; Amanda: Cynthia Blaise

William Shatner directed this one. Spock's long-lost brother shows up and things get out of hand.

1990

FUNNY ABOUT LOVE

PRODUCTION CREDITS: Directed by Leonard Nimoy; Produced by Jon Avnet and Jordan Kerner; Written by Norman Steinberg and David Frankel; Based Upon an Article by Bob Greene; Music Composed by Miles Goodman; Director of Photography: Fred Murphy; Costume Designer: Albert Wolsky

CAST ; Gene Wilder, Christine Lahti and Mary Stuart Masterson

Gene Wilder is a political cartoonist who falls in love with Christine Lahti and they marry. Their inability to conceive a child becomes a stumbling block in their relationship and they ultimately divorce, only to later reconcile. This a comedy drama which has neither enough good comedy nor enough good drama to be satisfactory and falls rather flat in spite of the best efforts of the director and the actors to overcome the limitations of the script. It's like they say, if it's not in the script it won't be on the screen.

1991

NEVER FORGET

(TV movie, first aired April 8, 1991)

Running time: 2 hours

PRODUCTION PRODUCTION CREDITS; Produced by Leonard Nimoy and Robert Radnitz; Directed by Joseph Sargent

CAST; Leonard Nimoy, Dabney Coleman, Blythe Danner

The true story of Holocaust survivor Mel Mermelstein, who successfully sued a racist group that offered a large cash reward for proof of the Holocaust (which they claim never happened) and then refused to pay up when Mermelstein offered his own evidence. The case was the first time the historicity of the Holocaust was noted as fact in an American court of law.

THE HISTORY OF TREK

The Complete Story of Star Trek from Original Conception to its Effects on Millions of Lives Across the World

James Van Hise

- *Star Trek VI*, the last Trek movie to star the original crew, will be released this winter
- By the author of *The Trek Crew Book* and *The Best of Enterprise Incidents: The Magazine for Star Trek Fans*

This book celebrates the 25th anniversary of the first "Star Trek" television episode and traces the history of the show that has become an enduring legend—even non-Trekkies can quote specific lines and characters from the original television series. *The History of Trek* chronicles "Star Trek" from its start in 1966 to its cancellation in 1969; discusses the lean years when "Star Trek" wasn't shown on television but legions of die-hard fans kept interest in it alive; covers the sequence of five successful movies (and includes the upcoming sixth one); and reviews "The Next Generation" television series, now entering its sixth season.

Perhaps no series in the history of television has had as much written about it as "Star Trek," but fans continue to snap up books and magazines about their favorite show. When the series first appeared on television in the 1960s, a book was already available chronicling its creation. And after the show was dropped three years later, people continued to write about it, actually increasing attention to the show until it returned in the form of a $40 million feature film in 1979.

Complete with photographs, *The History of Trek* reveals the origins of the first series in interviews with the original cast and creative staff. It also takes readers behind the scenes of all six Star Trek movies, offers a wealth of Star Trek trivia, and speculates on what the future may hold. A must for Trekkies, science fiction fans, and television and film buffs.

James Van Hise is the author of numerous books on entertainment, including *Batmania* and *The 25th Anniversary Lost in Space Tribute*. He lives in San Diego, CA.

$14.95, Trade paper, ISBN 1-55698-309-3
Television/Film, 25 B&W photos, 160pp, 8⅜ x 10⅞
Pioneer Books

TWENTY-FIFTH ANNIVERSARY TREK TRIBUTE

James Van Hise

- The Star Trek phenomenon is celebrating its 25th anniversary
- Written by the author of *The Trek Crew Book* and *The Best of Enterprise Incidents: The Magazine for Star Trek Fans*

Taking a close-up look at the amazing Star Trek story, this book traces the history of the show that has become an enduring legend. James Van Hise chronicles the series from 1966 to its cancellation in 1969, through the years when only the fans kept it alive, and on to its unprecedented revival. He offers a look at its latter-day blossoming into an animated series, a sequence of five movies (with a sixth in preparation) that has grossed over $700 million, and the offshoot "The Next Generation" TV series, which will be entering its fifth season as Star Trek celebrates 25 years of trekking.

Complemented with a variety of photographs and graphics, the text traces the broken path back from cancellation, the revelation of the show's afterlife in conventions, and its triumphant return in the wide screen in *Star Trek: The Movie*. He also looks at such spin-off phenomena as the more than 100 Star Trek books in print—many of them bestsellers—and the 50 million videocassettes on the market.

The author gives readers a tour of the memorials at the Smithsonian and the Movieland Wax Museums, lets them witness Leonard Nimoy get his star on the Hollywood Walk of Fame in 1985, and takes them behind the scenes of the motion-picture series and TV's "The Next Generation." The concluding section examines the future of Star Trek beyond its 25th anniversary.

James Van Hise who has authored such comics as *The Real Ghostbusters* and *Fright Night*, serves as publisher/editor of the highly acclaimed *Midnight Grafitti* and is the author of numerous nonfiction works, including *The Trek Crew Book*, *The Best of Enterprise Incidents*, *The Dark Shadows Tribute*, and *Batmania*. He lives in San Diego, CA.

$14.95, Trade paper, ISBN 1-55698-290-9
TV/Movies, 50 B&W photos, line drawings, maps, and charts throughout, 196pp, 8⅜ x 10⅞
Pioneer Books

Couch Potato Inc.   Las Vegas, NV 89130

TREK
The Next Generation

James Van Hise

● The *Star Trek* phenomenon celebrates its 25th anniversary as the new television series enters its fifth season

They said it wouldn't last, and, after its cancellation in 1969, it looked as if it wouldn't. But the fans refused to let it die and now *Star Trek* is thriving as never before. The *Next Generation* television series—entering its fifth year—continues the adventure. This book reveals the complete story behind the new series, the development of each major character, and gives plans for the future.

James Van Hise is publisher-editor of *Midnight Graffiti* and has written numerous books, including *The 25th Annniversary Lost in Space Tribute.*

$14.95, Trade paper, ISBN 1-55698-305-0
Television, B&W photos, 164pp. 8⅜ x 10⅞

Pioneer Books

THE COMPLETE LOST IN SPACE
Written by John Peel

The complete guide to every single episode of LOST IN SPACE including profiles of every cast member and character.

The most exhaustive book ever written about LOST IN SPACE.

$19.95...220 pages

Las Vegas, NV 89130 (702)658-2090

IT'S A BIRD, IT'S A PLANE
Written by James Van Hise

Few actors have so completely captured the public's imagination that when the name of the character he or she portrays is mentioned, that actor immediately comes to mind. Sean Connery is James Bond. Basil Rathbone is Sherlock Holmes. Clayton Moore is The Lone Ranger. And for 39 years George Reeves has been Superman! IT'S A BIRD, IT'S A PLANE examines the Superman television series, covering its 104 episodes in minute detail. Author James Van Hise provides a complete episode guide, interviews with Reeves' co-stars Noel Neill (Lois Lane), Jack Larson (Jimmy Olsen) and Robert Shayne (Inspector Henderson). In addition, the text includes complete cast biographies, a super-Superman quiz and a look at the George Reeves movie serial, THE ADVENTURES OF SIR GALAHAD, providing a guide to all fifteen chapters.

It's a bird...it's a plane...no, it's the greatest Superman book ever!

$14.95.................124 pages
Black and White Illustrations Throughout
ISBN#1-55698-201-1

IT'S A BIRD...
IT'S A PLANE...
NO IT'S THE...
TELEVISION
ADVENTURES OF
SUPERMAN

BY JAMES VAN HISE AND JOHN FIELD

$14.95/$19.95 CANADA   ISBN#1-55698-201-1   SCHUSTER AND SCHUSTER

The Green Hornet
Written by James Van Hise

Batman was not the only superhero television series to air in the 1960s. Its creators also brought ABC's THE GREEN HORNET, which starred Van Williams as the Green Hornet with martial arts superstar Bruce Lee as his sidekick, Kato, to the screen.

A guide to every episode of the television series, with actor and character profiles make this a complete look at this unique super hero.

$14.95...........120 pages
Color Cover, Black and White Interior Photos
SPECIAL OFFER: A limited edition volume combining the books on THE GREEN HORNET television series and the movie serial. This two-in-one book is only $16.95!

Boring, But Necessary Ordering Information!

Payment:

All orders must be prepaid by check or money order. Do not send cash. All payments must be made in US funds only.

Shipping:

We offer several methods of shipment for our product. Sometimes a book can be delayed if we are temporarily out of stock. You should note on your order whether you prefer us to ship the book as soon as available or send you a merchandise credit good for other goodies or send you your money back immediately.

Postage is as follows:

Normal Post Office: For books priced under $10.00—for the first book add $2.50. For each additional book under $10.00 add $1.00. (This is per indidividual book priced under $10.00. Not the order total.) For books priced over $10.00—for the first book add $3.25. For each additional book over $10.00 add $2.00.(This is per individual book priced over $10.00, not the order total.) These orders are filled as quickly as possible. Shipments normally take 2 or 3 weeks, but allow up to 12 weeks for delivery.

Special UPS 2 Day Blue Label Rush Service or Priority Mail(Our Choice). Special service is available for desperate Couch Potatoes. These books are shipped within 24 hours of when we receive the order and should normally take 2 to 3 days to get from us to you.

For the first RUSH SERVICE book under $10.00 add $5.00. For each additional 1 book under $10.00 add $1.75. (This is per individual book priced under $10.00, not the order total.)

For the first RUSH SERVICE book over $10.00 add $7.00 For each additional book over $10.00 add $4.00 per book.(This is per individual book priced over $10.00, not the order total.)

Canadian shipping rates add 20% to the postage total.

Foreign shipping rates add 50% to the postage total.

All Canadian and foreign orders are shipped either book or printed matter.

Rush Service is not available.

DISCOUNTS!DISCOUNTS!

Because your orders keep us in business we offer a discount to people that buy a lot of our books as our way of saying thanks. On orders over $25.00 we give a 5% discount. On orders over $50.00 we give a 10% discount. On orders over $100.00 we give a 15% discount. On orders over over $150.00 we giver a 20 % discount.

Please list alternates when possible.

Please state if you wish a refund or for us to backorder an item if it is not in stock.

100% satisfaction guaranteed.

We value your support. You will receive a full refund as long as the copy of the book you are not happy with is received back by us in reasonable condition. No questions asked, except we would like to know how we failed you. Refunds and credits are given as soon as we receive back the item you do not want.

Please have mercy on Phyllis and carefully fill out this form in the neatest way you can. Remember, she has to read a lot of them every day and she wants to get it right and keep you happy! You may use a duplicate of this order blank as long as it is clear. Please don't forget to include payment! And remember, we love repeat friends.

____Trek: The Lost Years $12.95   ISBN#1-55698-220-8

____Trek: The Next Generation $14.95   ISBN#1-55698-305-0

____Trek: Twentyfifth Anniversary Celebration $14.95   ISBN#1-55698-290-9

____The Making Of The Next Generation $14.95   ISBN#1-55698-219-4

____The Best Of Enterprise Incidents: The Mag For Star Trek Fans $9.95 ISBN#1-55698-231-3

____The History Of Trek $14.95   ISBN#1-55698-309-3

____Trek Fan's Handbook $9.95   ISBN#1-55698-271-2

____The Trek Crewbook $9.95   ISBN#1-55698-257-7

____The Man Between The Ears: Star Trek's Leonard Nimoy $14.95   ISBN#1-55698-304-2

____The Doctor And The Enterprise $9.95   ISBN#1-55698-218-6

____The Lost In Space Tribute Book $14.95   ISBN#1-55698-226-7

____The Complete Lost In Space $19.95

____The Lost In Space Tech Manual $14.95

____Doctor Who: The Complete Baker Years $19.95   ISBN#1-55698-147-3

____The Doctor Who Encyclopedia: The Baker Years $19.95 ISBN#1-55698-160-0

____Doctor Who: The Pertwee Years $19.95   ISBN#1-55698-212-7

____Number Six: The Prisoner Book $14.95   ISBN#1-55698-158-9

____Gerry Anderson: Supermarionation $14.95

____The L.A. Lawbook $14.95   ISBN#1-55698-295-X

____The Rockford Phile $14.95   ISBN#1-55698-288-7

____Cheers: Where Everybody Knows Your Name $14.95   ISBN#1-55698-291-7

____It's A Bird It's A Plane $14.95   ISBN#1-55698-201-1

____The Green Hornet Book $16.95 Edition

____How To Draw Art For Comic Books $14.95   ISBN#1-55698-254-2

____How To Create Animation $14.95   ISBN#1-55698-285-2

____Rocky & The Films Of Stallone $14.95   ISBN#1-55698-225-9

____The New Kids Block $9.95   ISBN#1-55698-242-9

____Monsterland Fearbook $14.95

____The Unofficial Tale Of Beauty And The Beast $14.95   ISBN#1-55698-261-5

____The Hollywood Death Book $14.95   ISBN#1-55698-307-7

____The Addams Family Revealed $14.95   ISBN#1-55698-300-X

____The Dark Shadows Tribute Book $14.95   ISBN#1-55698-234-8

____Stephen King & Clive Barker: An Illustrated Guide $14.95 ISBN#1-55698-253-4

____Stephen King & Clive Barker: Illustrated Guide II $14.95 ISBN#1-55698-310-7

____The Fab Films Of The Beatles $14.95   ISBN#1-55698-244-5

____Paul McCartney: 20 Years On His Own $9.95   ISBN#1-55698-263-1

_____Yesterday: My Life With the Beatles $14.95   ISBN#1-55698-292-5

_____Forty Years At Night: The Tonight Show Story   ISBN#1-55698-308-5 $14.95

_____The Films Of Elvis: The Magic Lives On $14.95   ISBN#1-55698-223-2

_____Batmania $14.95   ISBN#1-55698-252-6

_____Batmania II $14.95   ISBN#1-55698-315-8

_____The Phantom Serials $16.95

_____Batman Serials $16.95

_____Batman & Robin Serials $16.95

_____The Complete Batman & Robin Serials $19.95

_____The Green Hornet Serials $16.95

_____The Flash Gordon Serials Part 1 $16.95

_____The Flash Gordon Serials Part 2 $16.95

_____The Shadow Serials $16.95

_____Blackhawk Serials $16.95

_____Serial Adventures $14.95   ISBN#1-55698-236-4

_____Encyclopedia Of Cartoon Superstars $14.95   ISBN#1-55698-269-0

_____The Woody Allen Encyclopedia $14.95   ISBN#1-55698-303-4

_____The Gunsmoke Years $14.95   ISBN#1-55698-221-6

_____The Wild Wild West $14.95   ISBN#1-55698-162-7

_____Who Was That Masked Man $14.95   ISBN#1-55698-227-5

_____The Man Who Created Star Trek $14.95   ISBN #1-55698-318-2

_____Trek: The Making of the Movies $14.95   ISBN#1-55698-313-1

NAME:_____

STREET:_____

CITY:_____

STATE:_____

ZIP:_____

TOTAL:_____ SHIPPING_____

SEND TO: Couch Potato, Inc. 5715 N. Balsam Rd., Las Vegas, NV 89130